HOUNI

Forthcoming in the series:

and many more . . .

Hounds Of Love

Leah Kardos

BLOOMSBURY ACADEMIC
NEW YORK • LONDON • OXFORD • NEW DELHI • SYDNEY

BLOOMSBURY ACADEMIC
Bloomsbury Publishing Inc
1385 Broadway, New York, NY 10018, USA
50 Bedford Square, London, WC1B 3DP, UK
29 Earlsfort Terrace, Dublin 2, Ireland

BLOOMSBURY, BLOOMSBURY ACADEMIC and the Diana logo are
trademarks of Bloomsbury Publishing Plc

First published in the United States of America 2024

Bloomsbury Publishing Inc does not have any control over, or
responsibility for, any third-party websites referred to or in this book. All
internet addresses given in this book were correct at the time of going
to press. The author and publisher regret any inconvenience caused if
addresses have changed or sites have ceased to exist, but can accept no
responsibility for any such changes.

Whilst every effort has been made to locate copyright holders the publishers
would be grateful to hear from any person(s) not here acknowledged.

A catalog record for this book is available from the Library of Congress.

ISBN: PB: 979-8-7651-0699-0
ePDF: 979-8-7651-0701-0
eBook: 979-8-7651-0700-3

Series: 33 1/3

Typeset by Deanta Global Publishing Services, Chennai, India
Printed and bound in Great Britain

To find out more about our authors and books visit www.bloomsbury.com
and sign up for our newsletters.

Contents

Track listing

Side A – *Hounds Of Love*

Running Up That Hill (A Deal with God) (5:03)
Hounds of Love (3:02)
The Big Sky (4:41)
Mother Stands for Comfort (3:07)
Cloudbusting (5:10)

Side B – *The Ninth Wave*

And Dream of Sheep (2:45)
Under Ice (2:21)
Waking the Witch (4:18)
Watching You Without Me (4:06)
Jig of Life (4:04)
Hello Earth (6:13)
The Morning Fog (2:34)

Running time: 47:24

Acknowledgements

On 5 January 2024, shortly after I finished writing this book, Kate's former partner, bassist and sound engineer Del Palmer died at the age of seventy-one. His vibrant presence on *Hounds Of Love*, and many other Bush albums, will endure. May he rest in power.

This book owes a debt of thanks to Kate Bush fan communities past and present, especially those who contribute(d) to the *Homeground* fanzine and Gaffaweb archive, both of which have been invaluable points of reference. Special thanks to Professor Richard Kaczynski for his sage advice on all things esoteric. Stephen W Tayler and Sadia Sadia for their endless warmth. Tom Doyle for the friendly advice. Leah Babb-Rosenfeld at Bloomsbury for believing in me. Lexi Dick for still making and selling those beautiful dragon earrings.

Ben Dawson for being patient with me while I disappeared to write this. Liz Tray for being the best sub-editor with the best music taste in London. You were there every step of the way; I couldn't do this without you.

Finally, a special thank you to Albert McIntosh for convincing your mum to perform again in 2014. It was just fantastic.

Introduction

Hounds Of Love remains the most critically and commercially successful album of Kate Bush's career to date. It was released by EMI on 16 September 1985 and was the second album she had self-produced, the first recorded in her own studio. Structured to reflect the contrast between day and night, the more pop-oriented side A yielded four immaculate top 40 hit singles, 'Running Up That Hill (A Deal with God)', 'Cloudbusting', 'Hounds of Love' and 'The Big Sky', some of the best loved and most enduring compositions in the Bush catalogue. On side B, a hallucinatory seven-part song cycle called *The Ninth Wave* broke away from the pop conventions of the era, with strange and vivid production techniques that plunge the listener into the psychological centre of a near-death experience. Today, *Hounds Of Love* is universally considered a classic album, one of the defining high watermarks for art-pop production in the 1980s. Working at an unhurried pace in the creative safe haven of her newly built home studio at East Wickham Farm in Kent, Bush refined her production skills, elevating the hyper-expressive approaches that she had been exploring on her fourth album, and solo production debut, *The Dreaming* (1982), towards a more poised and accessible, yet still experimental and complex, pop aesthetic. With *Hounds Of Love*, Bush mastered the art of her studio-based songcraft, finally achieving full control of her work. When it came out, she was only twenty-seven years old.

As years pass, the album continues to accrue cultural value. Music publications like *Rolling Stone*, *Q*, *NME*, *Uncut* and *Mojo* have voted *Hounds Of Love* among the greatest albums of all time. In their 2016 retrospective review, Pitchfork gave the album a perfect ten out of ten, with critic Barry Walters lauding it as 'the *Sgt. Pepper* of the digital age's dawn; a milestone in penetratingly fanciful pop'.[1] In a 1985 interview with *Musician*, Bush said her newest album was 'the one I'm most happy with'.[2] Twenty years later, speaking to Tom Doyle for *Mojo*, she admitted that she still felt proud of how *Hounds Of Love* turned out, calling it, 'probably my best album as a whole'.[3]

It is significant that her 2014 London concert residency *Before The Dawn*, the artist's late, and so far only, return to live performance following a gap of thirty-five years from her last shows in 1979, the *Tour of Life*, had a setlist that included all but two songs from *Hounds Of Love* (the exceptions being 'The Big Sky' and 'Mother Stands for Comfort'). Nestled in the middle of a three-act structure, *The Ninth Wave* was presented in its entirety as an immersive, music-theatrical experience, fulfilling Bush's long-held aspiration to develop the piece in a visual direction ('for me, from the beginning, *The Ninth Wave* was a film. That's how I thought of it.'[4]) Those lucky ones in attendance at *Before The Dawn* could finally experience something of the artist's personal vision for the work. Bush's unexpected return to the stage saw fans from all corners of the globe making pilgrimages to the Hammersmith Odeon (known today as the Eventim Apollo, formerly the Hammersmith Apollo). It was the same venue where she performed the final *Tour of Life* show in 1979, which was, until that point, assumed to be the last show she would ever do. Tickets sold out in a matter of minutes, and as a result of the incredible amount of buzz the concerts generated, Bush saw eight of her albums enter the UK top 40 chart simultaneously, becoming the first woman to have ever done so. On this particular statistic, she reigns alongside rarefied male company: Elvis Presley (with twelve entries in 1977 following his death) and The Beatles (eleven entries off the back of their 2009 reissues).

To be tasked with writing this little book right now feels like a gift. Not only because Kate Bush is grossly overdue a volume in this series but also because *Hounds Of Love* has been experiencing a fascinating renaissance in popular culture. During the summer of 2022, 'Running Up That Hill' reappeared on the worldwide charts due to a sudden and dramatic surge in its popularity, sparked by a prominent sync placement in the fourth season of Netflix's flagship sci-fi fantasy series *Stranger Things*. 'Running Up That Hill' (or 'RUTH', as the artist herself later referred to it) became a global phenomenon. Within weeks of the first seven episodes being released on 27 May, it was clocking eight-million-plus streams per day. Across June and July, it was the most-played track in the world, twice topping the *Billboard* Global 200 and reaching number one spots in Australia, New Zealand, Switzerland, Sweden, Ireland,

Belgium, Lithuania and Luxembourg. Even though it was a significant hit in the UK back in 1985 (reaching number three), the song eclipsed itself in 2022, staying put in the number one spot for three weeks. 'Running Up That Hill' was named the UK's Song of the Summer by the Official Charts Company, and its latent success broke a number of Guinness World Records: the single that took the longest time to reach number one (thirty-six years and 310 days from date of release); at sixty-three, she became the oldest female artist to reach number one, snatching the title from Cher, who was fifty-two when 'Believe' hit the top spot in 1998. In a Christmas message posted to her website, Bush reflected on her 'crazy, roller coaster year', saying, 'I still reel from the success of RUTH, being the No 1 track of this summer. What an honour! . . . It was such a great feeling to see so many of the younger generation enjoying the song. It seems that quite a lot of them thought I was a new artist! I love that!'[5]

As I write, fans the world over continue to luxuriate in this gloriously late-flowering, unusually fruitful 'Kate Season'. In April 2023, there was a paperback reprint of her lyric collection *How to Be Invisible* (2018), with a random allocation of books containing messages from Bush handwritten in invisible ink (I refuse to test mine with a UV light, as I prefer to enjoy the infinite possibilities of my Schrödinger's Kate collectible). In June came the news that 'Running Up That Hill' had racked up yet another record, becoming the first solo recording from the 1980s by a female artist to surpass one billion streams on Spotify. In November, Bush was inducted into the Rock & Roll Hall of Fame.

She also announced in March that the physical distribution of her catalogue was being shifted from the mega multinational Warner Music Group to the comparatively tiny independent distributor and creative collective The state51 Conspiracy, known for its bespoke, limited editions. Freshly designed logos and visual assets for her Fish People label by Timorous Beasties (the Glasgow design studio led by Alistair McAuley and Paul Simmons) and Jonathan Barnbrook (the Grammy-winning graphic artist responsible for many of David Bowie's late-period album sleeve designs) feature across an entire physical re-release of her catalogue, with special vinyl editions available only from independent record stores and her website. In November 2023, Bush announced two 'special presentations' of *Hounds Of Love*. 'The Baskerville Edition' features a newly designed cover illustration of two dogs forming the shape of a heart and a special gatefold illustration of Bush with an embedded LED flashing light, powered by a small solar panel. The 'Boxes of Lost at Sea' are wall-mountable art pieces based on an earlier artwork Bush created for a 1994 auction for the charity War Child. She said of the original pieces, 'For many years I'd wanted to try and adapt that idea to include an LP . . . or two. The Fish People reissues on vinyl gave that design the chance to be reimagined.'[6] On her revamped website, two short promo films for the new editions appeared, written and directed by Bush, featuring child actor Gus Turner (*Ted Lasso*) and a voiceover by Sir Ian McKellen. The choice to reissue the catalogue might feel like a shrewd move given the sudden influx of younger fans coming into the fold, but it is also clear to see that these radically redesigned editions have been conceived and managed with a great deal of love and care.

The placement of 'Running Up That Hill' in the fourth season of the retro-nostalgic fantasy hit *Stranger Things* was an inspired choice. The music supervisor for the series, Nora Felder, didn't know that Bush was already a big fan of the show when she asked for permission to use the track.[7] Bush later spoke about her affection for the series in a rare interview on BBC Radio 4's *Woman's Hour* in 2022, saying, 'We watched [*Stranger Things*] right from the word go, from the first series onwards . . . I thought, what a lovely way for the song to be used in such a positive way, as a kind of talisman almost, really, for Max.' One of the main characters, Max Mayfield, played by Sadie Sink, is struggling with depression, grief and survivor's guilt over the death of her brother. Withdrawn and sullen, she listens to *Hounds Of Love* on her cassette Walkman on repeat, shutting out the world around her. When Max becomes trapped in the horrifying mindscape of a serial killer, her friends help her to escape by playing her favourite song ('Running Up That Hill'). Hearing it makes her remember the people in her life who love her, and in that crucial moment, she chooses to live. As the song reaches its ecstatic crescendo, Max makes her desperate run for freedom.

That moment was probably powerful enough by itself to boost the song's popularity, but 'Running Up That Hill' is an almost constant presence throughout the season – not only recurring in Max's storyline arc but also subtly sewn into the underscoring throughout. During the finale's key moment of brave confrontation, it appears again, enhanced by an epic, orchestral treatment. It's no wonder the song became an earworm for viewers. On the level of story and setting, the lyrics resonate meaningfully with the show's overarching themes of difference, specialness and empathy. Young outsiders, thrown into a perilous environment (whether the social nightmare of high school or the hellish parallel dimension of the 'Upside Down'), find that specialness is embodied in their difference, and bravery emerges from the trust and faith that they have in each other. *Stranger Things* can be enjoyed on multiple levels – as a note-perfect homage to horror in the style of *A Nightmare on Elm Street*, as a science-fiction adventure about a girl with psychic superpowers and her group of friends fighting evil in an alternate universe or simply as an allegory about the challenges of growing up: discovering who you are, who loves you and what you stand for.

That music can be a lifeline during dark times, a way to locate yourself when you feel lost, is a truth that many former weirdo outsider kids understand all too well. For some of us, it was Kate Bush's music that provided a place of refuge and a means of imaginative escape. In Fred Vermorel's biography, Bush is quoted as saying, 'school was a very cruel environment and I was a loner. But I learnt to get hurt and I learned to cope with it.'[8] Part of that coping mechanism was to retreat to her piano and inwardly explore turbulent emotive landscapes with chords, melodies, lyrics, voices, images. In an interview on TV series *Egos & Icons*, broadcast by Canada's MuchMusic channel in 1994, she referred to her music in terms of catharsis and friendship.[9] 'My music . . . it's a very private thing. And it's very much a release for me . . . it's like a very close friend.'

The contemporary resurgence of 'Running Up That Hill' was surely a confluence of many factors and not purely reducible to the lyrical and musical qualities of the song itself, stunning as they are. Part of it was immaculate timing: 2022 was a difficult year, beginning as it did in the grip of the Covid variant Omicron, with people reeling from the fog and fatigue of lingering lockdowns, tentatively re-emerging into a terrifyingly altered world at war. In our collective experience of that fear and uncertainty, with the forced separations, traumas and losses of the pandemic's stolen years, and in the face of a truly frightening ecological future, all the while we continue to be forced to navigate an increasingly toxic, socially and politically polarized reality, Bush's song of radical empathy, trust and determination felt like a tonic. But the song was only one part of a larger work of art that many newcomers would soon discover. *Hounds Of Love* is a journey through the beautiful and difficult terrains of vast and complicated emotional landscapes. Within it are songs of stubborn desire, bravery and cowardice, magical thinking, guilt and innocence, cold love, childlike joy, darkness and whimsy, self-doubt, surviving something extremely difficult and emerging on the other side of it stronger, wiser, transformed. It's a work of sweeping, thrilling ambition with a wealth of meticulous detail rendered in widescreen cinemascope – a work that was borne from a major work-life change that allowed the artist to write and record privately, in time with her own creative rhythms, returning to the same spaces where she sought emotional refuge in music as a child. Literate, musically elemental and atmospherically complex, the material strikes a balance between the accessible and strange, commercial and conceptual. Structures are confidently grounded in intensifying repetition and the whole is elegantly stitched together with subtle, recurring themes, familiar harmonic angles, imagistic echoes. The music and lyrics are supercharged by Bush's virtuoso vocal production and stunning use of the Fairlight CMI sampling synthesizer, with which she creates immersive soundworlds and sumptuous arrangements that combine the precision of cutting-edge music tech with the warmth and energy of rock and folk instrumentation. Familiar images return: pleading ghosts, sea, sky, night, land and dreamscapes; references to romantic literature; horror movies; books; Arthurian and folkloric symbolism; and uncanny animalia. The blackbird appears, a potent symbol that becomes a repeating reference in Bush's work from this point onwards. From the album art on the front and back covers, we recognize the correspondence between different points of view from above and below; with the stars in her hair and the sea around her legs, we see the female body in the water and of the air.

There has been a fair amount of writing on the life and work of Kate Bush over the decades, though the artist has always managed to retain her essential mystery. I won't waste the precious word count of this tiny book rehashing facts and details that are common knowledge. Bush's origin story – how she was marketed and overworked by EMI as their in-house oddball ingenue while still a teenager, and how she fought her way through many layers of patriarchal music-industry bullshit to wrestle control of her work – is an important context that this book will barely have the space to glance at. Instead, I have chosen to focus on

Kate Bush's emergence as a powerfully influential figure in music culture; a courageous experimentalist, a singularly expressive recording artist and a visionary music producer who, frankly, deserves more recognition for her aesthetic legacy. A woman who kicked some big doors down, making so much possible for everyone who came after her. Another aim of my writing is to focus on the experience of the album from the listener's point of view. The first chapter, 'Still dreaming', considers the growth and refinement of Bush's artistry during the early 1980s, and the inspirational and thematic threads from *Never for Ever* (1980) and *The Dreaming* (1982) that appear on *Hounds Of Love*. The second, 'I put this moment . . . here', tells the story of how the album was made, exploring Bush's studio practice, her pioneering use of music technologies, how she used the studio space as a songwriting tool and how she worked with musicians and engineers to execute her unique production vision. The chapters '*Hounds Of Love*' and '*The Ninth Wave*' examine each side of the record, track by track, exploring the ways in which this music can be meaningfully experienced. '*Before The Dawn*' considers how Bush carefully translated much of *Hounds Of Love* to a live format, creating a hybrid concert and musical theatre experience that offers a wealth of new detail which enriches our appreciation of the original source material. 'Wave after wave' considers the vast impact and influence that *Hounds Of Love* has had on music culture and creative practices through the years, underlining Bush's importance as a barrier-smashing, template-defying, business-smart, record-breaking, never-compromising role model for artists everywhere.

Hounds Of Love is a concept album that invites you to not only listen to it but also cross the boundaries of sensory experience into realms of imagination and possibility. What follows from here is my own reading of it, merely one of many possible readings. But here and now, with this little volume in your hand, it's just you and me. Let's exchange the experience.

The first woman

17 February 1978: Debut album *The Kick Inside* was released, going on to sell more than a million copies in the UK. Bush, aged nineteen, became the first woman in pop history to write a million-selling debut album.

11 March 1978: With debut single 'Wuthering Heights' (released 20 January), Bush became the first woman to have an entirely self-penned song reach number one in the UK chart.

2 April–14 May 1979: Bush was the first artist to use a headset with a wireless microphone. The innovation allowed her to sing and dance without having to hold a mic during the *Tour of Life*. This has since become commonplace in live performance.

20 September 1980: Bush's third album *Never for Ever* debuted at number one in the UK chart, making her, at twenty-two, the first woman to have ever done so with a studio album.

June 1986: In the 'Chartfile' column of *Record Mirror*, Alan Jones wrote, 'More than eight years into her chart career, Kate Bush [aged twenty-seven] has singlehandedly written all fifteen of her hit singles, a figure unrivalled by any other female singer/songwriter in the world.'

13 November 1993: Bush (aged thirty-five) wrote, directed and starred in what could arguably be called the first 'visual album' made by a woman, *The Line, the Cross & the Curve.*

6 September 2014: By the start of her twenty-two-night *Before The Dawn* residency, Bush (aged fifty-six) had eleven albums in the top 100, including eight in the top 40, setting a Guinness World Record for the most simultaneous UK top 40 albums by a solo female artist.

23 June 2022: Bush (aged sixty-three) set a new Guinness World Record for the longest gap between number ones on the UK's Official Singles Chart: forty-four years and eighty-three days from her debut single 'Wuthering Heights' to 'Running Up That Hill'. That record was broken in November 2023 when The Beatles hit number one with 'Now and Then', fifty-four years and 144 days since their last, 'The Ballad of John and Yoko', which came out in May 1969. Bush retains the record for the longest span between number ones by a solo female artist (forty-four years, 118 days). She also snatched the record for the longest time taken for a track to reach number one (thirty-six years and 310 days) from Wham! ('Last Christmas' took thirty-six years and twenty-three days).

7 July 2022: Bush became the oldest female artist to reach number one (sixty-three years and 342 days), knocking Cher, who had held the record for her 1998 hit 'Believe', off the top spot.

22 June 2023: 'Running Up That Hill' became the first solo recording released in the 1980s by a woman to pass a billion streams on Spotify. Bush was sixty-four.

Still dreaming

Albums are like diaries. You go through phases,
technically and emotionally, and they reflect the
state that you're in at the time.
– Kate Bush, *Rolling Stone*, 1994[1]

The leap in sonic and musical daring from the piano-led pop
of 'Wow' and 'Symphony in Blue' (*Lionheart*, 1978) to the
shattered shards of 'Babooshka' and the ammunition-click
percussion of 'Army Dreamers' (*Never for Ever*, 1980) were the
result of Kate Bush's conscious manoeuvring from one side
of the recording studio's glass divide to the other. *Lionheart*,
produced by Andrew Powell (with credited 'assistance' from
Bush), was rushed out in haste to capitalize on her first flush
of popularity in the wake of debut *The Kick Inside*, which had
come out nine months earlier. Like that album, *Lionheart*
drew heavily from the stash of songs, more than a hundred
demos,[2] that Bush had composed and recorded as a teenager.
Only three freshly written songs were added to the mix.
Without sufficient time to create an entirely new vision for
her follow-up, the artist later expressed, on several occasions,
her disappointment with how *Lionheart* turned out. The

reception from the press was cooler than anticipated, with the general critical consensus being that the album was an inferior repeat of her debut. Bush's dissatisfaction arose from being rushed, as she explained in a promo interview at the time. 'It was a difficult situation . . . I felt very squashed in by the lack of time and that's what I don't like, especially if it's concerning something as important for me as my songs are.'[3] Another big problem was her lack of power in the studio environment to realize her vision, as she reflected on in an interview seven years later:

> because I was a lot younger, and I didn't have the room and the space to be able to truly present my music . . . I wasn't powerful enough basically to be able to say, 'Look, I'm producing this myself. This is what I do.' . . . But you learn very quickly what you want. By the time the second album was finished, I knew that I had to be involved. Even though they were my songs and I was singing them, the finished product was not what I wanted . . . for me, [*Lionheart*] was not my album.
>
> – Kate Bush, *Keyboard*, 1985[4]

Never for Ever, Bush's third LP, came out in 1980, and it was the first album where she was credited for production duties, alongside co-producer and engineer Jon Kelly, Geoff Emerick's *protégé* and the trusted hand who had engineered *The Kick Inside* and *Lionheart*. In charge of her own arrangements for the first time, Bush used these new powers to summon a substantially larger ensemble than before – piano, of course, but now supplemented with a range of keyboard tones from Fender Rhodes, Yamaha

CS-80, Prophet and Minimoog synths. Her brother Paddy brought in a menagerie of acoustic objects that could be strummed, plucked and bowed – sitar, balalaika, koto, psaltery, mandolin, banshee, even a musical saw. She employed cutting-edge technologies that would come to define not only her own creative workflows but the incoming 'sound' of the 1980s: programmable rhythm machines like the Roland CR-78 and the Fairlight CMI (computer musical instrument), a revolutionary digital sampling synthesizer that Bush had probably first encountered when she contributed backing vocals on Peter Gabriel's third self-titled LP (the 1980 album often referred to as *Melt*, referencing the trippy, drippy, disfigured Polaroid of Gabriel on the cover by prog-adjacent graphic design collective Hipgnosis). Gabriel would soon become the first person in the UK to own a Fairlight and *Melt* and *Never for Ever* would be the first commercially released records to showcase the instrument at the start of the new decade. The Fairlight was an integral discovery that unlocked new ways of working and new creative possibilities for Bush, but being present to observe Gabriel's approach to studio production proved to be just as formative. On *Never for Ever*'s liner notes, Bush thanked Gabriel for 'opening the windows', perhaps a reference to *Melt*'s first track, 'Intruder', which begins with the line 'I know something about opening windows and doors'. In a creative sense, seeing Gabriel at work transformed the way Bush understood the role of the studio in her songwriting as a space that afforded both open-ended experimentation and meticulous control. Where *Lionheart*-era Bush suffered under the pressure to work quickly, *Never for Ever* Bush would take more time to get things right – more than five months were spent working on it, first at Air Studios and then Abbey Road, between September 1979 and May 1980. If getting an important detail right meant repeating a single take for a days, then that was what happened. Guitarist Brian Bath later recalled how, during his tracking sessions for 'Breathing', he 'must have played the same guitar bit 200 times . . . they must have gone through spools of tape.'[5]

'Breathing', *Never for Ever*'s climactic final track and its lead single, is sung from the perspective of an unborn child who is absorbing nuclear fallout through its mother's womb. The verse starts melodramatically with stark piano and voice, distant howling guitars and hesitant, stuttering machine-gun snare drums. By the time the chorus rolls around, the claustrophobic tension has given way to a gentle bath of lullaby Rhodes, throbbing synths and half-time ballad drums. Listening to it, we feel like we are floating helplessly beside her, trapped in that warm, poisoned place, breathing rhythmically 'out-in, out-in, out-in'. The song's extended bridge is a spoken radio-style broadcast describing the blinding flash of a nuclear bomb, after which the final, terrifying section begins as the in-utero baby becomes panicked and afraid. The music grows heavy with low overdriven guitars, crashing cymbals and Kate's escalating screams. At the apex of this crisis, a sharp filter sweep deadens the atmosphere and we are left suspended in a vacuum. Thirteen seconds later, a final bass note – a body slumping over – is left to stillness for another fifteen seconds of silence. The narrative approach to its production brought a new dimension to Bush's songwriting – now the sounds could immerse the listener, adding depth and detail to lyrical imagery, shared empathy and emotional experience. It was the moment on the album that Bush was most proud of. 'From my own viewpoint that's the best thing I've ever written', she told Kris Needs in *ZigZag* that year, adding, 'I call that my little symphony.'[6]

In a message to her fan club's newsletter in September 1980, the month of *Never for Ever*'s release, Bush expressed delight at how being in control of the production had allowed her songs 'to speak with their own voices . . . Every time a musical vision comes true, it's like having my feet tickled. When it works, it helps me to feel a bit braver.' *Never for Ever* was a tentative step towards self-production and bolder studio experimentation. Its songs possess some qualities of her earlier work, such as a reliance on piano-written material and the cosy AOR polish of late 1970s art-rock. But a newness is also present in the way they are dressed individually in sonic outfits that match their voices and personalities; like the horde of fantastical flying beasties escaping from under her skirt on the cover, *Never for Ever* hints that what we're hearing is only the beginning of what this artist is capable of.

Bush's bravery paid off. The album was a commercial success, scoring three top 20 singles ('Breathing', 'Babooshka', 'Army Dreamers'). It debuted at number one on the UK chart, making Bush (at age twenty-two) the first woman to have ever done so with a studio album. The success gave Bush the confidence to push even harder in an experimental direction with her next album, 1982's *The Dreaming*. In an interview with Rosie Boycott for *Company*, she compared the responsibility of self-production to motherhood, saying, 'as soon as you get your hands on the production, it becomes your baby', adding, 'you do everything for your own child'.[7] Indeed, Bush would end up giving more of herself than ever before to bring *The Dreaming* to life. The arrival of her fourth LP was not destined to be an easy birth.

Two months after the release of *Never for Ever*, the world was shattered by the murder of John Lennon. The start of the new decade was already fraught with anxieties about the future, and Lennon's killing felt like an axis shift, proof that nothing good comes from fame: you could devote your life to creating art and promoting peace and still be shot dead in the street. A few weeks after his death, Bush chose to play Lennon's '#9 Dream' (*Walls and Bridges*, 1974) among a selection of folk and world music on a New Year's Eve BBC radio programme hosted by Paul Gambaccini, song choices that hinted at the direction she might move to next. After six months of silence, the longest gap between releases in her career to date, the new single 'Sat in Your Lap' arrived in June 1981, reaching number eleven. It was finished and released early, while the remainder of *The Dreaming* was still a messy work in progress. Three months later, Bush told John Shearlaw at *Record Mirror* about her struggle with exhaustion, writer's block and 'a sort of terrible introverted depression' that had kicked in after the release of *Never for Ever*. The hard-hitting avant-tribal sound of 'Sat in Your Lap' was the result of a self-imposed 'shock' to Bush's usual working methods, using a drum machine and synthesizer alongside the piano to open up new rhythmic and sonic possibilities at the songwriting stage. She followed Gabriel's idea to remove all cymbals from the drum tracking and employed *Melt*'s engineer Hugh Padgham to help her get the rhythm parts down, even using the very same 'stone' room at Townhouse Studios, where he and Phil Collins had innovated their famous 'gated' drum sound on 'In the Air Tonight' (*Face Value*, 1981). The result was a surprising turn – the song is ferociously odd, sonically intense and relentlessly rhythmic in a way that Bush's music had never been before. A breakthrough. She told *Record Mirror*, 'the single is the start, and I'm trying to be brave about the rest of it . . . I want it to be experimental and quite cinematic, if that doesn't sound too arrogant.'[8]

The rest of *The Dreaming* came together, painstakingly and expensively, over the next fifteen months with many long sessions across multiple studio spaces – the Townhouse, Abbey Road, Odyssey and Advision Studios, while, for 'Night of the Swallow', sessions with Irish composer Bill Whelan, his band Planxty and members of The Chieftains were hosted at Windmill Lane Studios in Dublin. At one point, the sessions had spread out to occupy all three studios at Abbey Road simultaneously. As production rolled along, the personnel list continued to expand. Padgham, who was not entirely on-board with Bush's vision and in demand elsewhere, decided to leave, and engineers Nick Launay and Haydn Bendall were brought in. They were open to Bush's wild ideas involving corrugated iron-wrapped drum shells, aerosol cans, smashed marble, crowds of people, Paddy's runaway bullroarer and TV's animal impersonator, Percy Edwards. The songs remained elusive, changing form and direction constantly, shifting in character as new details were added. Bush adopted a responsive method, listening and adapting to her creations as their personalities and voices sounded clearer and truer with each creative decision.

Meanwhile, EMI were becoming impatient with how long it was all taking, and they were getting twitchy about the mounting studio costs. Towards the end of 1981, Bush admitted to feeling a bit lost and overwhelmed with her unwieldy project, saying, 'I've worked on this album so intensely for so long that I seemed to be losing sight of my direction. I really wasn't sure what to do next – and that has never happened to me before.'[9] She took a break to gather her thoughts and finalize the lyrics, and at the end of 1981, she made a rare appearance at Sotheby's annual rock memorabilia auction, picking up a perspex sculpture of John Lennon and Yoko Ono in their famous 'Two Virgins' pose and a copy of the shooting script for The Beatles' *Magical Mystery Tour* film. Perhaps it was *Magical Mystery Tour*, with its bold, imagistic studio textures, or the troubling spectre of Lennon's recent death that served as inspirational guideposts for Bush as she navigated the final phase of *The Dreaming*, which took place over a marathon stretch of sessions at Advision between January and May 1982 with mix engineer Paul Hardiman and Bush's partner, and bass player, Del Palmer alongside for support. Her approach to vocal performance involved the embodiment of multiple character roles and their distorted emotional perspectives. In voicing these characters to life, she used the extremities of her range and physical ability via whispers, guttural growls, animal sounds, shrieks and throat-shredding screams. Dramatic, often unpretty affectations that sounded worlds away from the girly 'sweetness' associated with her earlier work. The final vocal recordings, which took weeks, were then edited and mixed along with the whole project over many months spent in a windowless basement room at Advision. According to Hardiman, the process involved 'hours of crippling tedium with occasional bursts of extreme excitement.'[10] At the time, Bush said it was 'the hardest thing I've ever done . . . even harder than touring! It was worrying, very frightening, but at the same time very rewarding.'[11] The vibes during the final stretch were reportedly strange. Bush was said to be surviving on joints, grapes and tea; Palmer compared the basement studio to being trapped in a submarine; Hardiman took to wearing a ginger wig and roleplaying a character called 'My Dad' to help lighten the mood; the three of them occasionally donned polystyrene cup ear cones to help focus in on the sound.

When it was finally complete, EMI came close to rejecting it outright. Brian Southall, who was then head of press, told *Uncut* in 2014, 'That was the closest EMI got to returning an LP in my time. The trouble was, you couldn't go back to Kate and say, "There's no three-minute pop single on here." She'd say, "I know, I didn't write one!"' It was Bush's most expensive album to date, not only in terms of the studio hire costs but also in the price she paid for pushing herself to the limits of physical and mental exhaustion. The title track, released as the second single, stalled in the charts at number forty-eight, the first commercial disappointment in what had been a strong streak of hits since the turn of the decade. A third single, 'There Goes a Tenner', reached number ninety-three. The fourth, 'Suspended in Gaffa', failed to chart.

Her friend Peter Gabriel had also met similar resistance with *Melt*; Atlantic Records dropped him from their roster after hearing early mixes (though the A&R who suggested this, John Kalodner, realized his mistake a few months later and resigned Gabriel for his new workplace, Geffen). Gabriel reflected on this decades later in an interview with *Q*. 'I thought I'd really found myself on that record and then someone just squashes it. I went through some primordial rejection issues.'[12] Gabriel's fourth self-titled LP (known as *Security*) took nearly as long to record as *The Dreaming*, and both records were released the same month, September 1982. Both relied heavily on the Fairlight for tactile textures, fusing futuristic timbres with traditional folk and Indigenous musical elements, and both explored extreme expressive edges of the human voice, with lyrics that probed the darker corners of the human psyche. Both albums would lay the groundwork and establish the aesthetic grammar of their breakthrough artistic and commercial successes to come, *Hounds Of Love* in 1985 and Gabriel's *So* in 1986. *The Dreaming* was undeniable proof of Bush's skill as a self-producing artist and represented a clean break from her previous persona – the swirly costume-box girl from the *Tour of Life* and the albums that preceded it. For Gabriel, the turbulent, experimental nature of his work in the early 1980s didn't harm him in terms of critical reputation. By contrast, Bush was dragged by the UK music press.

Steve Sutherland for *Melody Maker* declared 'Sat in Your Lap' an 'arthritic, artistically constipated, out-of-touch travesty'.[13] The pseudonymous Red Starr at *Smash Hits* called it 'every tackily acted piece of melodramatic Bush rolled into one ghastly mess'.[14] Rose Rouse at *Sounds* expressed her 'revulsion at the over production' on *The Dreaming*, adding, 'I'm drowning in a sea of vocal overdubs',[15] and Neil Tennant, reviewing 'There Goes a Tenner' for *Smash Hits*, sniffed, 'Very weird . . . Obviously she's trying to become less accessible.'[16] A few critics conceded admiration for Bush's audacity; for example, Chris White, writing for *Music Week*, dubbed *The Dreaming* 'her most weird and wonderful album to date, distinctly uncommercial', adding, 'Bush is still the most creative female artist on the UK pop scene'.[17]

The reaction in the United States was more positive, perhaps in part due to EMI's choice not to release *Lionheart* and *Never for Ever* there, giving *The Dreaming* a bigger impact. *Record* called Bush 'the only female rocker out there doing anything original (or experimental)'.[18] Michael Davis in *Creem* pointed out, 'no one who closes an album braying like a donkey can be accused of being too pretentious, now can they?'[19] Back in the UK, EMI were feeling less sympathetic. The singles had tanked. Radio play had dropped off. Gamely, Bush hit the publicity trail, appearing on the BBC's flagship music and talk shows *The Old Grey Whistle Test* and *Pebble Mill at One*, children's TV (ITV's *Razzmatazz*) and radio programmes at home and in mainland Europe. At the same time she was out selling the record, EMI wound down their promotional campaigns and admitted defeat. In interviews from around this time, one can sense the fatigue and frustration underneath her gentle decorum at being asked to explain *The Dreaming* in digestible soundbites to a media that had already decided not to support her work. Often, she had to field questions about why her new album wasn't commercially appealing or as successful as her earlier efforts. When Gabriel went on *Whistle Test* to promote *Security* in October 1982, he seemed to be afforded a measure of respect denied to Bush when she'd appeared on the same show three weeks earlier. The hosts Mark Ellen and David Hepworth didn't treat Bush's work with the same seriousness, instead asking her mundane questions about Australia and if she knew how didgeridoos were made.

By the time her publicity commitments had run their course, Bush was completely burnt out. Yet despite how difficult the process was, and the stinging reception it received, the experience of creating *The Dreaming* had been an affirming and fulfilling one. Years later, she reflected:

> It was probably the most difficult stage I've been at so far . . . and for the first time I felt I was actually meeting resistance artistically . . . but it was important that it happened to me because it made me think, 'Right. Do I really want to produce my own stuff? Do I really care about being famous?' And I was very pleased with myself that, no, it didn't matter as much as making a good album.[20]

She remained pleased over the years, citing *The Dreaming* as a personal milestone – a rare moment when she felt artistically satisfied. Bush had upheld the promise she made to herself after the disappointment of *Lionheart*. Through sheer bloody-minded determination, she had done what she set out to do. Navigating the sacred spaces of power usually only accessible to men, she had arrived as a producer. She had survived. As the years passed, the world slowly woke up to the delirious genius of *The Dreaming* and the realization that it was a sonic artefact ahead of its time. Its influence can be felt in the sample-based experimentation of Art of Noise, the overloaded cascading glossolalia of Elizabeth Fraser's vocal work with Cocteau Twins and with the cacophony of hard-hitting percussion and vocal layers on Public Image Limited's *This is What You Want. . . This is What You Get* (1984) and *Album* (1986). As Simon Reynolds noted in *The Guardian* in 2014, regarding the reception to Bush's next record, *Hounds Of Love*, 'As the postpunk era gave way to the glossy, overproduced 80s, suddenly Bush's sumptuous soundscapes made more sense than they had during the era of 2 Tone and Joy Division . . . With bands such as the Banshees and the Bunnymen opting for lavish orchestrations, Bush now seemed less like a throwback to pre-punk times.'

Threads of continuation

When you listen to Kate Bush's albums from the first half of the 1980s back to back, there is a sense of momentum that builds from *Never for Ever* to *The Dreaming* and further on to *Hounds Of Love*. Production becomes braver, the sound progressively specific, detailed and refined. Lyrical themes continue to mine deeper, darker recesses of human experience and there is the continued fusion of ancient and modern, nostalgic and futuristic, the push and pull of 'then', 'when' and the 'now' riding in on the curl of the wave. Complex emotions are presented prismatically, refracting through stories of survival, transformative fantasy, textural dreamscape and sonic-cinematic hauntings.

Bush's three-year retreat from public view after *The Dreaming* was not an act of contrition. It was the opposite, a doubling down. The complaint from EMI that her way of working was too expensive? Solved. She'd build her own studio. Leaving the stifling atmosphere of London, Bush and Palmer relocated to a seventeenth-century farmhouse near Sevenoaks, Kent. She oversaw the construction of her new creative refuge, a 48-track recording facility built in a barn on her parents' property, East Wickham Farm, her childhood home. Now in closer proximity to her family, tucked away from the eyeballs of the media and having recently acquired her very own Fairlight, Bush had manifested the ideal conditions to begin working on what would become *Hounds Of Love* ('I wrote the songs for this album in a tiny room overlooking endless fields. I could see the weather coming for miles . . . '[21]). Working at a much more relaxed pace, Bush maintained a low profile; she didn't even share the music with record company executives until it was completed. Its outstanding commercial performance ended her battles with EMI for creative control. Many years later, in a 2005 interview for *Mojo*, she still seemed tickled about the win: ' . . . it was an enormous hit, it was so fantastic. [Cups hand to hear] Sorry, what's that you said? Sorry? Didn't want me to produce it? They left me alone from that point. It shut them up.'[22]

When *Hounds Of Love* was released, some commentators picked up on the threads of continuity from *The Dreaming*. Only a month after featuring Bush in a snide 'Where Are They Now?' article, *NME* had to admit that what marked *The Dreaming* as a failure was now distinguishing *Hounds Of Love* as a runaway success. 'Musically and lyrically Kate Bush's influences haven't changed since *The Dreaming* and its three brilliant singles ("Sat in Your Lap", "The Dreaming", "There Goes a Tenner") bombed. Only the climate has changed, i.e.

the BBC and a nation of reactionary punters are now ready for our Kate's weird shit.'[23]

Many techniques that Bush employed on *The Dreaming* reappear on *Hounds Of Love*. Gabriel's no-cymbal rule remains in effect and the tribal, percussive rhythms that energize songs like 'Sat in Your Lap', 'The Dreaming' and 'Leave it Open' play a central, unifying role on *Hounds Of Love*. Where on *The Dreaming* structural sections often arrive with a dramatic shift in tone, like the light relief of Bush's 'concierge' in the bridge of 'Get Out of My House' or the sparse piano verses studded around the rollicking, Irish folk-inspired choruses in 'Night of the Swallow', on *Hounds Of Love* the rhythms drive forward relentlessly with a rumbling intensity, rarely changing shape and never deviating from their fixed course. The Fairlight remains a source of inspiration, not only with its ability to render any sound musical but also with its uncanny on-board sounds that rubbed up against traditional acoustic instruments in interesting ways. As Bush described to *Keyboard*, 'the combination of very acoustic, real sounds and very hard, electronic sounds is fabulous. I like to create contrasts and extremes for the atmosphere that you're building around a particular song.'[24] The deliberate fusion of contemporary and traditional instruments, a distinguishing feature of *The Dreaming*, is an approach that is further explored and refined on *Hounds Of Love*.

When Bush writes away from the piano, the harmonies and musical structures she comes up with feel like a dramatic departure from her early, flowery style, and this is one of the primary qualities that defines her unique sound in the early-to-mid-1980s. The grounded drone that forms the basis of 'The Dreaming' is suggestive of vast Outback landscapes and an atmosphere of ancient magic. The teetering balancing act between the two chords of 'Watching You Without Me' is miles away from the restless harmonic jumping of her early songwriting style. Bush's production practice becomes a form of sonic cinematography, from the jungle foliage and sticky humidity of tracks like *The Dreaming*'s 'Pull Out the Pin' to the sustained evocation of water, ice, weather and ocean waves on side B's narrative-driven song suite, *The Ninth Wave*.

Longstanding themes of life, death and the human instinct to survive, from the panicked foetus in 'Breathing' crying out for a future to the Vietnamese soldier's internal scream of 'I love life!' as he prepares to kill to save his own in 'Pull Out the Pin', come to the surface in a powerful way across *The Ninth Wave*. The thread of songs that speak of ambition, impatience and growing up – *Never for Ever*'s 'All We Ever Look For', *The Dreaming*'s 'Sat in Your Lap' and 'Suspended in Gaffa' – reach a crisis point on *Hounds Of Love*, where young people find themselves on the cusp of maturity; afraid of love, unable to communicate clearly, daughters and sons protected from reality by the unquestioning love of mothers and the magical thinking of fathers. The long line of spectres that haunt Bush's catalogue, from Cathy's ghost at the window in 'Wuthering Heights' to the spirit of the dead 'Houdini' making contact from beyond the grave, suggest the possibility of love's power to transcend death, or alternatively, its power to trap a poor soul forever in a limbo of frustrated longing and heartbreak. *Hounds Of Love* draws all of these themes and fears to the crest of the wave with an appropriate measure of gothic excess: images of heroines in peril, tales of terror, witches on trial, spirits in limbo, bodies trapped under ice, little lights and dark depths, mothers, fathers, life, death and rebirth. Discovering who you are, where you belong, how to love better. Finally growing up.

From dove to dragon

If one were to put Kate Bush's first twenty singles in a line-up, from 'Wuthering Heights' all the way to 'Cloudbusting', one might notice the songs becoming increasingly idiosyncratic and emotive. Simon Reynolds described this evolution as being 'almost unrivalled for sustained brilliance and escalating oddness', adding that he considered 'only the Beatles, from start to finish, and Bowie, from "Space Oddity" to "Fashion", [to] surpass it'.[25] For Bush, the progression reflected a process of artistic becoming, which she explained to Peter Swales in a 1985 interview for *Musician*:

Swales: Once an album finally exists, can you enjoy it?

Bush: I couldn't with the first two albums as they didn't turn out the way I wanted them to . . . But the third and fourth albums, yes, I could listen to those and be quite critical about them and yet feel quite pleased about some of the things on them. Artistically, I was especially pleased with *The Dreaming* . . . The new album [*Hounds Of Love*] is the one I'm most happy with.

On the front cover of her debut *The Kick Inside* (1978), nineteen-year-old Kate Bush is pictured clinging to the bars of a large painted dragon kite. Photographer Jay Myrdal remembered meeting the young artist. 'When I shot the photographs for Kate no one had heard of her. She was very young and even EMI didn't expect her first album to be anything more than a minor success.'[26] Bush appears helpless, as if she has been tied to a mast, offered as bait. On the back cover, Palmer's drawing of a man on a kite contains the secret KT symbol – the detail that has been hidden on every album Bush has released.

The album's in-flight cover, inspired by a scene from *Pinocchio* (1940) where Jiminy Cricket glides past a whale's vast eye, would become a potent visual metaphor for Bush's meteoric rise to fame. It also evokes the lyrics of 'Kite', the fourth track: 'I'm like a feather on the wind / I'm not sure if I want to be up here at all'. As Myrdal intuited, no one at EMI expected Bush's kite to soar the way it did. She found herself strapped in for a wild, exhausting ride, one that she wasn't sure she wanted to be on.

There were two music videos created to promote 'Wuthering Heights'. In the 'white dress' version, she wears dove-shaped earrings, cut from mother of pearl. She wore them many times that year; you can spot them in photos and TV appearances. She also put them on for her live TV debut on *Top of the Pops*. The figure of the flying bird sits well alongside the kite symbolism. Onwards, Bush would continue to draw upon the imagery of flying creatures: dressed as a bat on the back cover of *Never for Ever*, the swallow with broken wings from *The Dreaming*, *The Ninth*

Wave's drowning blackbird. I enjoy wondering about those dove earrings. Were they worn with intention, perhaps as a talisman of calm, or protection? In 1985, she chose to wear silver dragons – heavy metal, sharp-edged and gothic – for the amethyst-themed *Hounds Of Love* cover shoot and was also seen wearing them in other photoshoots and in public around the time of the record's release. She wore them during her *Top of the Pops* appearance performing 'Hounds of Love' in 1986. Dragons are mythic creatures, linked to forces of chaos, wisdom and magic. Compared to the wide-eyed child with the dangling doves, the woman with the gleaming dragons seems far more confident, knowing . . . and powerful.

I put this moment . . . here

The production of *Hounds Of Love* was strikingly original for its time: poised, elemental, ethereal. And it's worth taking a moment to shout about how this unique sound was innovated by a woman and created during a time when very few female music creators had access to hi-tech recording equipment and facilities. USC Annenberg, a university in Los Angeles, surveyed a decade's worth of data – from Grammy nominations and *Billboard*'s Hot 100 charts (2012–21) – and found that women accounted for 14.4 per cent of songwriters and only 2.8 per cent of producers.[1] Music studio and production cultures have always been, and remain, male-dominated. It's difficult to find hard statistics on the gender gap in the mid-1980s, but we can safely assume that the situation would not have been any better. Across the broad history of music, sisters have always had to do it for themselves.

In 1982, Yoko Ono's self-produced album *It's Alright (I See Rainbows)* and Siouxsie Sioux's involvement in the experimental production of the Banshees' *A Kiss in the Dreamhouse* and *Feast* (1983) by The Creatures shared a kinship with *The Dreaming*. Not only in the sense that they were made roughly around the same time, similarly flirting with avant-garde, electronic and art-pop aesthetics, but also because they are visionary works directed by female songwriters who seized control of production as a means of expressing complex ideas. When Kate Bush hit a new commercial peak with *Hounds Of Love*, she had virtually zero female peers doing it the way she was. The only other comparable artist at that time, in terms of autonomous working methods, creative control and access to studio resources, was Prince.

With her new 48-track recording facility, Bush had brought her music back to her childhood home, back to the very barn that had housed a mice-infested pump organ she had played as a young girl. She recreated it as her ideal working environment, a space that granted the artist more privacy and control over her creative process than ever before.

A studio of one's own

At East Wickham Farm, her father, Robert, helped Bush and Palmer manage the construction of the new recording studio, which was completed by the start of 1984. Its design suited Bush's preferred ways of working. Purposefully, there was no line of sight between the control room and recording spaces; communication was made through walls via mic and foldback monitors, an agreeable setup for an artist who did not enjoy being watched while she worked. The control room was large and comfy like a living room, decorated in blue wallpaper with fluffy white clouds – an accommodating space to work long hours in. Windows let in natural light, views of gardens, trees and sky. The tracking setup consisted of a Soundcraft 2400 series mixing desk, alongside two 24-track Studer tape machines, which were synced together with a Q Lock 310. Forty-eight tracks might sound like a lot of layers, but for an artist as texturally minded and detail-oriented as Bush it was a minimum requirement, as she told *Keyboard*. 'Even if it's for a vocal idea, 24 tracks doesn't seem to go anywhere with me.'[2] Monitoring was handled by a pair of AMS (Advanced Music Systems) speakers, powered by an Amcron amplifier. The recording room was furnished with a Grotrian-Steinweg grand piano. Shuttling between the studio and her eight-track home demoing setup were her prized Fairlight CMI (purchased towards the end of *The Dreaming*), a second sampler, an E-Mu Emulator, and her favoured synthesizer, a Yamaha CS-80 (the polysynth also favoured by Vangelis that was famously featured on his score for 1982's *Blade Runner*).

The outboard equipment in the control room housed a range of dynamic processing options: Urei 1176 and 1178 compressors, Drawmer and VP Gate Keeper II noise gates, Scamp filters, A&D F760X-RS compressor/expanders. All of these units were essential for keeping the dynamics in control, especially for vocal performances that could surge from whisper to scream and back again in the space of a single note. They were also needed to achieve those huge, Padgham-style gated drum sounds that Bush was so fond of. There were racks full of reverb effects: AMS units, an obligatory Lexicon 224 (the legendarily lush digital reverb, one of the most desired sounds of the 1980s) and Bush's favourite, the Quantec Room Simulator: 'It's got a kind of coldness . . . a true feeling of being in different places.'[3]

Having unlimited access to the facility was crucial. Not only did it minimize the financial outlay (studio time for *The Dreaming* reportedly racked up costs at around £90 per hour, that's about £375 per hour in today's money, thousands per day multiplied over a recording period of twenty-one months), it also gifted the artist with time and access to the tools and technologies she needed. Bush explained to *Melody Maker*, 'Knowing the astronomical amount studio time cost used to make me really nervous about being too creative. You can't experiment forever, and I work very, very slowly. I feel a lot more relaxed emotionally now that I have my own place to work.'[4]

No longer reliant on moving her project from one London studio to another nor forced to work with different teams of people at different locations, the bulk of the album was conceived and created with only Bush and Palmer in the control room. Palmer, who assisted with engineering on many of Bush's records from *Hounds Of Love* onwards, has been quick to downplay the importance of his role in Bush's creative process when asked. In a 1993 interview, he said, 'I probably have more involvement than anybody else in what she does . . . I say that very modestly because I don't really feel that anybody has that much involvement in what she does, it all comes out of her own head.'[5] He told *Sound on Sound* that sometimes Bush would work in the studio alone without an engineer present, saying, 'I was able to just set her up with a sound, and she'd take care of it herself. She'd record all the vocals, then phone me up and say, "Let's put it all together".[6]

Stocked up on knowledge gained from the brutal experience of creating *The Dreaming*, Bush's approach on *Hounds Of Love* was more careful and direct. Her working methods had previously involved multistep processes that seemed to erode the fidelity of her initial inspirations: first, sketching the song idea in private, then producing a rough demo (at home on her eight-track) to share with players so they could develop their parts; the last step would involve building the song from the ground up across multiple laborious studio sessions. The process for *Hounds Of Love* was sleeker and more economical, preserving the spontaneous energy of those initial inspirational sparks. Bush explained,

> All the tracks on this album are what were originally put down as demos turned into masters . . . It's an old story really, but recreating the atmosphere of those demos is virtually impossible. I was determined this time to make that all part of the process. It affects the whole attitude towards recording because you've actually got the thing there, and you're just filling it in.[7]

This 'filling in' was achieved with layers of performances on top of, and around, the bones of the demo. Much of this was performed by Bush, on her sampling synthesizers, and a string of individual musicians who were invited to the studio, one at a time, to complement the material already in place.

Her instructions for the visiting musicians were often very specific. For the tracking of 'And Dream of Sheep', Irish folk musician John Sheahan performed the final phrase on tin whistle over and over for several hours until she found the exact 'bend' in pitch she wanted. Martin Glover (aka Youth, an original member of Killing Joke and later a renowned producer), who contributed bass to 'The Big Sky', later reflected on Bush's process.

> She has a very clear idea of how she'd like to direct the scene at any time. She commands a great respect in the room and everybody is clearly looking at her to lead . . . She let me do what I liked, she gave me some direction, then said, 'Thanks very much, off you go'. Then she chopped it up and arranged it in the Fairlight. I learned a lot from that, how to put a record together.[8]

There are hardly any guitars on *Hounds Of Love*, but when they do appear, they make a big impact. Alan Murphy, who played on the *Tour of Life* in 1979 and previously appeared on *Never for Ever* and *The Dreaming*, provided lacerating embellishment to the driving textures of 'Running Up That Hill' and contributed to the propulsive groove of 'The Big Sky'. He assisted Bush in composing the threatening rhythmic bed of 'Waking the Witch', working under her direction to flesh out ideas over a skeletal outline of LinnDrum samples and handclaps. The track would finally take shape with synth sequences programmed by Kevin McAlea. The other guitarist on *Hounds Of Love* is just as impactful in an atmospherically inverse way. Australian classical guitar virtuoso John Williams dapples sunlight across 'The Morning Fog', a warmth that suggests the possibility of an uplifting conclusion for the troubled protagonist of *The Ninth Wave* at the end of their ordeal.

When it came to bassists, Palmer would take on some of the work ('The Morning Fog', 'Jig of Life' and 'Running Up That Hill', and Fairlight bass on 'Waking the Witch'), but other players would be invited to lend their distinct personalities to the project: Youth ('The Big Sky'), Pentangle's Danny Thompson ('Watching You Without Me') and ECM star Eberhard Weber, who had played on *The Dreaming*'s 'Houdini' ('Mother Stands for Comfort', 'Hello Earth').

The tracking of *Hounds Of Love* in the studio was a slow, incremental process, not reliant on the collective synergies of group collaboration but rather on careful, individual selection. As Palmer explained, '[it] was very much a case of getting the right person for the right thing on the right track.'[9] For the musicians involved, it would have felt more like being woven into the fabric of an elaborate tapestry and nothing like being in a band at all. An exception was taken for the Irish interlude on 'Jig of Life', which was arranged by Bill Whelan and tracked with members of Planxty at Windmill Lane Studios in Dublin.

Bush's sparing approach with musicians might have been influenced by the Fairlight, which afforded her a method of working out arrangement ideas in an approximate way before committing real musicians to the task. 'You have a whole barrage of different sounds that can spark off ideas and really develop the final arrangements I consider myself very lucky because I'm a keyboard player . . . Now [with the Fairlight] I can compose parts I never could before at the keyboard – it lets you get so much closer to the whole song.'[10] An example of this new affordance can be heard in the spiky chamber-pop arrangement of 'Cloudbusting', a minimal palette of live string sextet, Fairlight and percussion arranged so deftly that the addition of more traditional rock or pop instrumentation would destroy the balance. 'Under Ice' is comprised of similar flourishes but created exclusively with Fairlight sounds. She told *Keyboard*, 'What really gets me about the Fairlight is that any sound becomes musical. You can actually control any sound you want by sampling it in, and then being able to play it . . . the amount of potential exploration you have there with sounds is never-ending, and it's fabulous.'[11] Bush had been exploring the potentials of noises-as-music since the smashed glass of 'Babooshka' and across *The Dreaming*, but on *Hounds Of Love* sound-sampling is deployed with more restraint and narrative purpose, for instance with the contained violence of 'Mother Stands for Comfort' and the sound of the wind, rendered melodic and musical at the closing moments of 'Hello Earth'. Where uncanny, sampled Fairlight and Emulator tones dominate, they are given space to speak. The two tones used on the opening of 'Running Up That Hill', the frozen background drone and the lead riff, while sounding completely different, actually originate from the same Fairlight factory preset, 'TRAMCHLO'. The melodic riff uses a version of sound that is tweaked with a subtle pitch envelope on the attack of the note. For the ambient background, it was elongated with a long, icy Quantec Room Simulator reverb tail, then lowered and slowed by processing it through a tape machine at half-speed. The effect of these sounds in combination is a heightened sense of tonal coherence, a shared strangeness that feels otherworldly-organic. On 'Watching You Without Me', Bush does a similar trick, taking a single Fairlight sample to create interlocking melodic figures, patterns interacting in a delicate, teetering limbo while Thompson's slippery double bass ducks and dives, and sumptuous orchestrations by Michael Kamen surge, curl and subside. For Bush, there was no rule around the Fairlight and LinnDrum sketches being replaced with real players or not; rather, she would wait for the songs to 'tell [her] what to do'[12] once the lyrical and vocal ideas had crystallized.

Another technology that significantly contributes to the album's personality is the LinnDrum, the sample-based percussion sequencer that revolutionized rhythm in the mid-1980s. It offered an alternative to live drums and allowed musicians to programme their own patterns. It also sounded like a beast compared to Roland's weaker-sounding analogue 808 and 909 drum machines, especially when beefed up with signal processing from the Eventide Harmonizer and AMS reverb. The LinnDrum programming on *Hounds Of Love* is credited to Palmer, who would input the patterns verbally dictated by Bush. Usually done at the initial songwriting stage, these parts served as the rhythmic foundations upon which the song's scaffolding would be constructed. Describing the process of composing 'Running Up That Hill', Bush recalled, 'I asked Del to set a Linn pattern – I sung him the part – and he got that together and we set that to play the pattern round and round, and I worked out the vocal that would go over the top.' That starting point would make it to the final version of the song with very little embellishment. 'We got Stuart [Elliott, drummer] in, and because the Linn pattern was so full in itself it was just a matter of him sticking a snare down.'[13] Although the LinnDrum carries much of the rhythmic weight, Elliott, who had played on every Bush album to date, was called in to bolster the Linn layers with extra detail across seven of the twelve tracks. For 'Cloudbusting', Bush would ask both Elliott and Charlie Morgan (who played on *Lionheart*) to summon a militaristic wall of marching percussion. She also combined their performances to achieve the heavy, beating heart of 'Hounds of Love'. Morgan also contributed to 'The Big Sky', 'Waking the Witch' and 'Jig of Life'.

Back to nature

Another significant addition to Bush's production arsenal was the acquisition of a Nagra recorder. Nagras were the industry-standard portable sound recording systems for films, TV and radio. The units could be taken outside to record environmental sounds, and that's exactly what Bush wanted to use it for. Specifically, to capture natural sound effects for *The Ninth Wave*.

> The second side of the album has a theme running through it and there were lots of sound effects we had to get . . . Trying to get a bit of sea is unbelievable. We got in sound effects albums but they're awful – so noisy, or it's the wrong kind of sea. I'd never really thought about the wrong and right kind of sea before, but as soon as you put it in context with the track you suddenly realise there's all different kinds of sea.
>
> – Kate Bush, *International Musician and Recording World*, 1985[14]

Bush used these production techniques to flesh out her lyrical images with realistic, natural details, applying sound to the canvases of her songwriting much like a painter building a vivid, textured world with layers of oil. The evocation of the natural world – the 'rain-making' cloudbuster, the cracking thunder of the heart, finding the right kind of sea, with gulls calling from above and the faint echo of whale song in the depths below – are far from trivial or indulgent sound effects. They are world-building and immersive. An expressive dimension in Bush's production that is deeply, romantically connected to nature.

This painterly approach feels allied with the style and ethos of the Pre-Raphaelite Brotherhood, the short-lived Victorian art movement that sought to fuse realistic depictions of the natural world with romantic subjects drawn from religion, myth, literature and poetry. Speaking at a fan convention in 1990, Bush admitted that paintings had been 'quite influential' on her work, adding, 'when I was very young I was into Millais's pictures . . . Do you know "The Huguenots"?' The artwork she was referring to was *A Huguenot, on St. Bartholomew's Day* (1852) by Sir John Everett Millais, arguably the most well known of the Pre-Raphaelite painters. Earlier in her career, Bush acquired a large painting that, she claimed, had 'cost me all the money I had once'. A morbid parody of Millais's most famous piece *Ophelia* (1851–2), it depicts the image of a drowned, broken doll floating past a flooded gutter. 'A lot of people find it disturbing but I don't. I lived with it for ages. Looked at it every day.'[15] Millais's *Ophelia* imagery is evoked in John Carder Bush's photograph of his sister on the back cover of

Hounds Of Love, the artist floating in dark water, surrounded by weeds and flowers. Carder Bush later reflected on the image:

> I was on a scaffold hanging over the pool . . . the warm water that was poured in from the kitchen tap looked black and menacing. Ophelia and The Lady of Shalott [of Tennyson's poem] flitted across the scene and then it was that rescue me, take me back into the world, no, don't rescue me, leave me here look that makes it so fascinating and memorable.[16]

Millais was only twenty-two when he painted *Ophelia*, working for months in the countryside near Hogsmill River, Surrey, composing the background flowers, boughs and water-rat infested reeds with painstaking detail. The doctrine of the Pre-Raphaelites, which upheld the importance of the artist's private interpretations and agency, had four guiding rules: (1) artists must have genuine concepts to express; (2) they are attentive to nature, to better know its expression; (3) they favour what is direct and heartfelt, excluding what is conventional and given and (4) they produce good work. At the 1990 convention, Bush went on to say, 'I would love to be able to paint. Particularly in oils . . . The sense of detail and colours, it's so alive. I would love to be able to do something like that.' But, of course, her productions are exactly like that.

Bringing her creativity back to the family nest at East Wickham Farm was a significant move. The place where Bush had taught herself to play and write songs as a child was a locus of power that drew her back. *Hounds Of Love* bears the warm influence of her family; Paddy's textural ideas and musicianship, John's poetry; their parents' unwavering support, wisdom and care for her wellbeing. It is significant that each of their voices can be heard somewhere on the album.

It wasn't only Bush's immediate family who brought the easy atmosphere of home life to *Hounds Of Love*, her extended family in Ireland also played a role. Her father, Robert, was from Essex, but Bush's mother, Hannah, was raised in rural Dungarvan, County Waterford. She came from a deeply musical family, a household where people from the town would gather to dance and play music together. During the making of *Hounds Of Love*, Bush and Palmer, who also had a familial Irish connection, travelled to Dublin to record instrumental parts for 'Jig of Life'. The pair also went south to reconnect with extended family, who, according to Palmer, 'seemed to come out of the woodwork there were so many . . . "This is cousin Mick, this is cousin Johnny . . . " There were thousands of them.'[17] Most of the lyrics for *Hounds Of Love* were finished in Ireland, as the pair explored the edge of the Dingle Peninsula, Kerry's windswept coastline at its most dramatic with craggy cliffs, wide salty skies of threatening weather, jagged rocks jutting out of the ocean, sheep grazing on rolling hills that edge towards the pounding waves of the Atlantic Ocean. Unhurried, Bush spent a few months soaking up the pastoral spirit of her ancestral home. 'It was a tremendous elemental dose I was getting, you know, all this beautiful countryside. Spending a lot of time outside and walking, [the music] had this tremendous stimulus from the outside.'[18]

When it was time to put the final vocals on tape, Bush, who had been a night owl on *The Dreaming*, developed a preference for singing during the day, telling *Musician*, 'The *Dreaming* was much more of a night-time album . . . on [*Hounds Of Love*] I tended to do them in the afternoon when it was sunny because the atmosphere was right.'[19] In that same interview, she admitted to getting into an altered state ('just a little drunk') to psych herself up for some of the more dramatic vocal moments on 'The Big Sky' and 'Waking the Witch' ('the hardest thing for me is to be able to feel relaxed enough to be uninhibited').

Final vocals were tracked with Palmer, who dished out the details on how Bush's bright and present vocal tone was achieved to *Sound on Sound* in 1993. He claimed the approach hadn't changed much since *The Dreaming*: a Neumann U47 microphone would be positioned in a reflective live room with stone walls and bricked flooring; that sound would then be processed through an 'overdose of compression', with a noise gate engaged to clean up the spill. Bush would move away from the mic to breathe and managed her distance based on the volume of her performance. Palmer admitted this was a messy approach, but they loved the results. 'From a purely technical standpoint, it's really badly done, there's just so much compression on everything. But I'm not interested in being technical, I just want it to sound good, and if it does, then what's the point of changing it?'[20] A big part of Bush's vocal sound on *Hounds Of Love* has to do with how she, as a singer, works creatively with lively room sound and over-compression by varying her performance style, often mid-lyric. For example, the spiky, declarative high register notes in the verse of 'Hounds of Love' are loud enough to catch reflections in the live room, yet Bush's voice swiftly melts into an intimate, low croon at the end of the phrase without diminishing in volume or losing focus in the mix. This technique can also be observed in the relatively exposed vocal of 'And Dream of Sheep', where forcefully delivered lyrical images ('chasing white horses') are led towards resolution with lines that are barely voiced at all ('let me be weak').

Hounds Of Love was completed during a final stretch in the summer of 1985 with mix engineers Brian Tench and Julian Mendelsohn. The process was a carefully calibrated affair, involving Bush's copious notes (Palmer: 'You should see the notes! There's two files, this thick! . . . you'd never believe it') and the choreographed movements of three or four sets of hands on the Soundcraft's faders to achieve the final mix. Bush would even assert control over the mastering stage. Engineer Ian Cooper, who had also mastered *The Dreaming*, recalled being handed a list of notes for *Hounds Of Love* so long that it rolled onto the floor.[21]

> There were times I never thought it would be finished. . . . But I did love it, I did enjoy it and everyone that worked on the album was wonderful. And it was really, in some ways, the happiest I've been writing and making an album. And I know there's a big theory that goes round that you must suffer for your art, you know, 'it's not real art unless you suffer'. And I don't believe this, because I think in some ways this is the most complete work that I've done, in some ways it is the best and I was the happiest that I'd been compared to making other albums.
> – Interview with Kate Bush, BBC Radio 1, 1992[22]

With *Hounds Of Love*, Bush's craft as a producer turned towards mastery. It is the significant mark on the map of her career where her technical prowess rose to meet the demands of her exacting artistic vision. Her unique and sensitive approach to the production of *Hounds Of Love* is one of the reasons it endures, and it still sounds utterly remarkable today, nearly forty years after it came out.

Hounds Of Love

Kate Bush is pictured resplendent, bathed in amethyst organza, with her family's Weimaraner dogs (Bonnie and Clyde) resting in her arms. Her hair is fanned out as though she is floating on water while the light ripples on the fabric underneath her in swirling, dreamy waves. Around her head, and visible through her hair, are pink and silver sequins that shine like stars. Her face is made up in cool tones of lilac, blue, pink and coral; in her hair, there's a conspicuous streak dyed pale purple. The look on her face is sensual, slightly sleepy, elegantly guarded. The dogs on either side recall the image of Hecate – the Greek goddess of the threshold realms, the places where crossroads meet – with her hounds.

Hounds Of Love is a purple album, not only with its cover imagery but also in overall sound and atmosphere: lush, mysterious, tonally dark. According to the Maitreya School of Healing, co-founded by Bush's friend, the late healer Lily Cornford (the addressee of the song named after her on Bush's 1993 album *The Red Shoes*), this colour ('wisteria amethyst') promotes strength, dignity, spiritual growth and courage. Squared and set at a distance by a thick white frame, the ideas and colours of the album inside are forecast:

water, sky, storms, stars, the dream world, the liminal place between life and something else; chill and warmth; power and restraint. Never has Bush appeared so soft and so strong.

'Restraint' is probably not a word that had been used to characterize Bush's aesthetic up until this point; however, the first side of *Hounds Of Love* (which is self-titled) features a collection of songs united by a remarkable sense of musical economy and precision. Of course, Bush was under pressure from EMI to have another hit, especially in the wake of *The Dreaming*'s relatively disappointing reception. But it would be incorrect to assume that *Hounds Of Love* was a calculated attempt at recapturing mainstream success. The album sounds different because it was built differently. Its new sense of simplicity and immediacy, especially with the four singles taken from side A, could be attributed to Bush and Palmer's newfound mastery of sequencing technologies. The LinnDrum could be programmed with user-defined two-bar rhythmic patterns, which could then be arranged into songs and stored in the unit's onboard memory. This led to a more or less continuous rhythmic element forming the bedrock of new songs. Palmer was a dab hand at programming the LinnDrum with the rhythms Bush could hear in her head ('I would get Del to manifest in the rhythm box the pattern that I wanted'[1]). Similarly, the Fairlight's built-in sequencer, 'Page R' (or Real Time Composer), enabled Bush and Palmer to arrange looping sections of music inside the instrument itself. Across side A, the sequenced patterns keep the music firm and consistent, focused, locked in. Ostinatos and stubborn grooves stretch out and dominate. Washes of harmony drone in place or repeat in short cycles. Colour, variation, drama and dynamic interest are achieved by decorative live-played embellishment, the intensification of drums, percussion and vocal textures, and melodic dissonances that grind against the rails of the songs' rigid, programmed pathways.

This pattern-based structural coherence is matched by tonal, melodic and harmonic continuities across the set. Bush moves elegantly through the tonal centres of each song like a chess grandmaster – C natural minor ('Running Up That Hill') to F ('Hounds of Love'), F ('The Big Sky') up a third to A minor ('Mother Stands for Comfort'), up another third to C# minor ('Cloudbusting'), setting us up perfectly on the edge of darkness for the beginning of side B, aka *The Ninth Wave*. On side A, there are melodic angles and shapes that recur, chord progressions that are recycled, structural *idée fixe* motifs carefully woven into the fabric of the whole. Lyrical themes work standalone, but also together, taking meaningful shape around ideas of love, relationships, family, innocence and the end of childhood. Phonic echoes connect the yelping dogs of 'Hounds of Love' and the howls of 'Mother Stands for Comfort'. 'I hid my yo-yo' from 'Cloudbusting' speaks to the affirmative 'yeah yeah yo' of 'Running Up That Hill', which also bubbles up in the ecstatic vocalizations of 'The Big Sky' ('looking at the yeah yo, yeah yo, yeah yeah yeah yeah yeah-yo') and the final moments of clarity on 'Hounds of Love' ('I need love love love love love, yeah yo, yeah yo, yo(ur) love'). Yes, *The Ninth Wave* is the crowned conceptual piece of *Hounds Of Love*, but there's still a lot of interesting world-building going on here on side A.

'Running Up That Hill (A Deal with God)'

The first thing you hear is the Fairlight drone (the half-speed TRAMCHLO preset, drenched in thick, Quantec reverb haze), sounding two notes a third apart (C and E♭). The drone fades in, already eternal and unmovable, and it remains present, a spectral, azimuth flow that never ends or changes; it only fades away once everything else in the song has finished its work. The next thing you hear is the eager, thundering beat, a combination of LinnDrum rhythms and Stuart Elliott's muscular toms and snare. Deeper than usual, the kick sample is tuned so low (around 65Hz) that it practically functions like a bass, drowning out Palmer's playing and grounding the track in a relentless, hungry gallop that dominates the texture. Within the taut grid of drum sounds, Elliott's stray toms ricochet towards the left, like the rattling clickety-clack of a heavy train. The hook comes in on an otherworldly Fairlight lead, meowing the outline of the melodic confines of the song to come. One of the sources of musical tension in the song is the way Bush pushes against these boundaries, which is confined to a single octave. She will often hit the roof of the phrase (B♭) with an insistent, almost combative energy, like a bird testing a glass ceiling for a way out (for example, in the agitated movement between two pitches on the line: 'Do you want to know, know that it doesn't hurt me').

The tonality of the song isn't firmly established until Fairlight pads, supporting the melodic hook, resolve to C natural minor at the end of the first phrase. The main chord progression in the verses (and mostly throughout) is a

sliding ascending movement over three chords: VI - VII - i
(A♭ - B♭ - Cm). This progression is echoed in other minor
mode songs elsewhere on the record; we'll hear it again in
'Cloudbusting', 'And Dream of Sheep', 'Under Ice' and 'Hello
Earth'.

As the harmonies twist and wrap around the unbending
drone, Bush's melodies make the most drama of limited
options. Less of a flowing arc and more of a polygon shape, a
song line leaps over intervals of minor 7ths, minor 6ths and
open 5ths, her voice hitting the target notes with forcefulness
and precision. At the end of the verse, Bush switches to a more
caressing voice and the first softening melodic curve, 'Do
you want hear about the deal that I'm making?' Throughout
the song, these moments of strident, declamatory intervallic
leaping are briefly surrounded by softer movements of lyrical
warmth ('You, it's you and me'). The syncopated three-note
background phrase ('yeah yeah yo') doesn't move with the
rest of the music to the tonic (C minor), but rather skips
down to the flattened 7th (B♭); similarly, during the chorus
– an 'ee-yo' that sticks awkwardly on the second degree –
both dissonances contribute to an overall sense of focused,
stubborn insistence.

Paddy Bush's balalaika, a Russian instrument similar to a
mandolin, crashes into the texture of the chorus, his tremolo
sounding brittle and sharp, bursting into a shimmering,
eternalized version of the glittering shards of smashed reality
at the end of 'Babooshka'. The harsh angles of the chorus,
repeating the cutlass intervals of the hook (leaping minor
7ths, minor 6ths and perfect 5ths), draw beauty from the
underlying harmony, shading the A♭ chord with a major

7th on the word 'could', underlining a sense of longing in the lyric.

The bridge section (at 2'48") introduces an edgy, impatient guitar rhythm from Alan Murphy as the ensemble of Bush voices plead, 'C'mon baby, come on darlin', let me steal this moment from you now'. With the words 'Let's exchange the experience, ohh', the voices hold strong on an uncomfortable cluster while Elliott's tom fill breaks like thunder through a cavernous six-second reverb, after which Bush's voices collapse with a moan. From this cataclysm onwards, dangerous elemental forces are at work in the track. Murphy's volatile guitar screeches and wails, Elliott's thunderous toms continue to peal, Bush's voices writhe, twist and lurch in the background, as if in pain or ecstasy. Her lead vocal maintains focus throughout with unflinching, controlled yearning, throwing sparks of human heat against the rumbling momentum. As the excitement begins to die down, Bush sings the final lines of the song in dual voices, one pitched down to a man's range. The transformation is achieved, the song is complete.

The lyrics speak of the desire to swap places with a romantic partner to fully understand their experience and point of view. Bush explained to *The Times*: 'It seems that the more you get to know a person, the greater the scope there is for misunderstanding . . . So what that song is about is making a deal with God to let two people swap place[s] so they'll be able to see things from one another's perspective.'[2] It is also clearly a song about penetrative sex, expressing the desire to swap that physical experience, to know how it feels to be a bottom ('Do you want to know that it doesn't hurt me') or a top ('Unaware I'm tearing you asunder'). To understand what it feels like to dominate and be dominated. And from here, experiencing the powers of a man's body, Bush knows that many of the challenging aspects of life will be easier. Getting to where she wants to go – running up that road, up that hill, even up a building – will pose no problems. The notion of gender being a kind of superpower will be touched on again in the lead single of her next album, 1989's *The Sensual World* ('Now I've powers o'er a woman's body, yes'). Here, the transgression of the binary experience creates space for genuine empathy and equality. Growth comes from experience, and experience irrevocably alters how we think and understand ourselves. The song is empowered and empowering without being selfish, and not at the expense of kindness and generosity. It resonates down through generations of shifting social norms and gender politics. In Bush's discography to this point, she had sung from the perspective of an unborn child, an undead ghost, a man, woman and donkey. She even performed in male drag during her 1979 Christmas special ('Ran Tan Waltz'). But with these final pitch-mangled lines, this was the first time Bush had sung in the voice of an evolved, empowered, non-binary entity.

The accompanying music video, directed by David Garfath, shows Bush and her dance partner dressed in identical grey Japanese hakama trouser-skirt outfits. Her co-performer, soon after the video was shot, began her gender transition and is now named Misha Hervieu, adding a rather remarkable extra component to the subversive nature of the lyrics. Outstanding choreography by Diane Gray, formerly of the Martha Graham Dance Company, has Hervieu lifting and manipulating Bush's body into various shapes and positions, and as they interact, they mirror and clash in movements that resemble an elegantly balletic form of wrestling. Bush, who does not mime to the song, gestures the drawing of a bow and arrow (mirroring the photo by John Carder Bush that was used for the cover of the single) before the pair lose each other in a crowd of strangers wearing masks of their faces. The final shot shows both dancers standing apart, each preparing to shoot their arrow. The video was intended to be Bush's farewell to dance ('It was sort of saying goodbye to that dancing side of me . . . I feel very much a shift now from dance into film imagery'[3]). In 2023, on her website, she reflected, 'I hoped "Running Up That Hill" could be seen as a filmic piece of dance.' Bush was only twenty-five when she composed and demoed the song in late 1983. It is an ethereal pop masterpiece that grabs you by the body with esurient momentum. A mature and focused articulation of desire and an elemental scream for equality. It creates empathy, not only for the others that we love, but also for our multiple other selves, hidden deep within.

'Hounds of Love'

Announced with a sample from Jacques Tourneur's black-and-white occult classic *Night of the Demon* (1957) (Bush: '[the film was] a real favourite of ours'[4]), with a petrified-sounding Maurice Denham shouting, 'It's in the trees! It's coming!', thick layers of thudding, adrenaline-drenched beats (combined takes of double-stick drumming from both

Elliott and Morgan) kick into gear. The beat, made up of toms and kick drums only, captures the panic of a chase with an asymmetrical 3+3+2 cross-rhythm loop that places early syncopated emphasis on the backbeat, giving the rhythm a jumpy, perilous-but-infectious velocity. A similar jumpiness is evident in the lyrical prosody of the verse, which crams the line into the space of two beats ('when-I-was-a *child* running-in-the *night*', 'hiding-in-the *dark* hiding-in-the *street*'), echoing the shape and urgency of the similarly rushed 'If-I-only *could*' line from 'Running Up That Hill'. As in the previous track, the drums dominate the texture, and the drum sound is maxed out even further here by the use of gated compression tricks that Bush and Palmer had gleaned from Hugh Padgham during the Townhouse sessions for *The Dreaming*: setting microphones up at a distance from the drum so as to pick up an amount of indirect sound from the room, then, according to Morgan, 'compressing them like mad, really crunching the sound up . . . this ridiculous blanket of percussion'.[5]

Through the centre, the harmonic spine of the track is another continuously flowing Fairlight wash, not a drone this time, but a 'Page R' looping chord sequence that differs slightly between verse (three chords, F - C/F - B♭/F) and chorus (four chords, Dm/F - F - B♭/F - C/F). The chords are bright, major, hyper-alert, with a layer of Fairlight strings pulsing in the background with pin-sharp staccato. From the first chorus (at 0'40" with the words 'Here I go'), the texture becomes pinned down by an unchanging root note, played by cellist Jonathan Williams. His rhythmic staccato obsessively saws away on the ragged edge of F, not quite a bass line and not quite a drone, but bringing a useful amount of brusque, excitable Bernard Herrmann-style horror score energy to the table. For the first chorus, he's on the left side, then moves to the right for the second verse, extending his rhythm across bouncing octaves. By the final chorus, he's there on both sides, like the panting of the hounds that are getting ever closer. Like Prince's 'When Doves Cry', 'Hounds of Love' is a pop oddity without a bassline, and like that song, the lack of low-frequency instruments serves to highlight the elegance and power of its simple, intricately calibrated production. The primary elements at play are Bush's voice, the pounding rhythm from the drums and the gnawing tension of the cello holding everything down with a fraying string.

But the mood isn't entirely sinister; there's room for playfulness. A slightly hiccupping Buddy Holly/Cyndi Lauper affectation in Bush's voice, the mighty *THHRROWW* of her shoes into the lake with the baying hounds yelping the counterpoint line – as she laughingly explained to Tom Doyle, 'the backing vocals, the doggy "ow, ow, ow" . . . it's the "Hounds of Love", innit?'[6] The lead vocal's trajectory rides on waves of tension and emotion, again with wide, angular intervals (leaping across perfect 4ths, 5ths and octaves). Phrases in the verses start with top-down declarative motion ('When I was a child', 'I found a fox', etc.) that naturally wind downwards to Bush's solemn-sultry register ('Now hounds of love are hunting'). Where there is courage and affirmation in the lyric, phrases tend to bubble upwards in pitch ('Oh here I go!', 'Do you know what I really need?'). As the lyric turns towards self-understanding in the final sections, and the singer realizes that the very thing they need is the thing they are running away from, the vocal begins to frolic around the melodic space. Bush swoops and twirls through extended lines in the outro ('I don't know what's good for me, I need love love love love love love, yeah-yo, yeah-yo, your love'), as though she has discovered that the dogs chasing her just wanted to play all along. 'It's not about wanting the "Hounds of Love" to catch you and tear you apart. That's what you think they're going to do. But they might want to catch you and lick you and play a game and be friendly dogs.'[7]

Some of the lyrical imagery in 'Hounds of Love' appears to have been drawn from another postwar film, Michael Powell and Emeric Pressburger's folkloric melodrama *Gone to Earth* (1950), based on the 1917 novel of the same name by Mary Webb. Set in the 1890s Shropshire countryside, the story concerns a superstitious, animal-loving girl who adopts a wild fox cub as a pet and ends up hotly pursued by a wealthy, fox-hunting squire. The tragic story illustrates the dilemmas of female freedom, autonomy and entrapment within the confines of male desire. Keeping the cinematic references coming, the music video for 'Hounds of Love', which Bush directed herself, took inspiration from Hitchcock's 1935 spy thriller *The 39 Steps*. In it, Bush is dragged by the arm, at speed, by a man from her workplace through a dark forest. They end up at a music hall where she accepts being handcuffed to him, and they dance in a locked ballroom style around the room before escaping together.

'Hounds of Love' sits at the head of the table of similar songs that Bush has written about being trapped by love – a recurring theme in her music since 'Wuthering Heights' and 'Oh to Be in Love' from *The Kick Inside*. Many pop songs before and since have tackled the topic of not wanting to be tied down by a relationship, but 'Hounds of Love' has the maturity to understand that love is a high-risk reward, and loving requires bravery and vulnerability. We can feel an instinct to run away from the thing we really need to face. It's an exquisite anthem for the commitment-phobic that encapsulates something very honest about the ambivalence and intensity of romantic desire.

'The Big Sky'

From Bush's account, 'The Big Sky' was a difficult composition to pin down, going through at least three vastly different incarnations before settling into its final form. '[It] gave me terrible trouble', she said in an interview at the official fan convention in 1985, adding, 'it was just one of those songs that kept changing – at one point every week'. She mused, 'Maybe it was all to do with what the song is about, the fact that it's changing all the time, like the sky, always changing!'[8]

Getting the song just right was important because 'The Big Sky' is one of the crucial pins holding *Hounds Of Love* together. Across the introduction, we hear a section of music that plays only once, offering a glimpse of the rainmaking to come on 'Cloudbusting' and also hinting at its militaristic drum beat and pulsing Fairlight string textures. There are more prophetic visions contained in the song's lyrical descriptions of clouds – one in the shape of Ireland (hinting at the ancestral 'Jig of Life' on side B) and another that warns of an impending flood ('This cloud says, "Noah, c'mon and build me an ark'") that leads to *The Ninth Wave*. 'Hello Earth' might be referring back to these moments in 'The Big Sky' when Bush sings of being 'there at the birth', 'out of the cloudburst, the head of the tempest'. The song draws its power from the forces that drive *Hounds Of Love*: big weather and big rhythms.

The first piano notes of the album are heard when the song kicks in proper at 0'16", accompanied by an elemental kick-snare beat, Morris Pert's rumbling percussion and Youth's gangly slap-bass. From here, the track builds incrementally in an extended, steady crescendo that only breaks once, briefly, to pause for the passing jet. Wide, jangly acoustic guitars enter at 0'36", before the now familiar Fairlight string wash at 0'55". By 1'30" Murphy has contributed an edgy, circular guitar motif, and Morgan and Palmer are frantically clapping, flamenco-style, on the 16th rhythm (panned cleverly far left and right; on headphones, the effect is an enlivening, brain-tickling jostle). Add some tambourines and Paddy Bush's droning didgeridoo, and it's a party. And we haven't even gotten to the throng of Bush voices (referred to in the song as 'sisters') that come out to play.

Once again, the harmonic underpinning is simple and repetitious, remaining in the same F major territory as 'Hounds of Love', but here with a mixolydian flavour (mixolydian mode is like a major key but with a flattened seventh degree). The movement between F and Eb/F (I and bVII/I) repeats, builds and intensifies, powering the track towards a dizzy, hyperventilating climax.

Bush's lead vocal is delivered with charming childlike innocence; its phrases have exuberant *naiveté* ('And if you're coming, *JUMP!* 'Cause we're leaving with the big sky!') and mock-pouting petulance ('You never understood me, you never really tried'). Again, the melodies employ leaping intervals and angular turns. Significantly, the main hook is built around a perfect 5th (upwards from F to C, and back down to F again, 'the big sky'). The songs up to this point have teased and played with this shape, but 'The Big Sky' is the first one to hammer the motif home. It will recur, woven into the verses of 'Cloudbusting', rising with the opening notes of 'And Dream of Sheep', oscillating in limbo during 'Watching You Without Me', falling downwards over the closing moments of 'The Morning Fog'.

In the ad-libbed sections over the coda, Bush pulls a range of surprisingly uninhibited noises from her body, and that's saying something for a vocal made in the wake of *The Dreaming*. The performance reaches a point of manic-ecstatic fervour with guttural moans, elastic whistle-tone screams and a full gospel-style choir of Kates, suggesting a connection between heavenly paradise and the pleasures of nature and childhood imagination. The spirited, church-like atmosphere of the track not only resonates with the evocation of Noah, his ark and the deal he made with God, but its brightness and positivity provide extreme contrast to the occult-related terror of 'Waking the Witch' on side B.

Under Bush's direction, the video for 'The Big Sky' looks and feels as madly joyous as the track sounds. Wearing a silver suit, she is seen sitting on a *Mary Poppins*-style London rooftop, holding binoculars, with a backdrop of constantly changing weather, playing a variety of roles. As the song builds, so does a raucous crowd of characters in costumes associated with flight: jet fighter pilots, astronauts, superheroes. Bush's brothers and many of the musicians featured on the song appear in the video alongside around 100 specially invited fans and, by the end, two giraffes, because, why not? Their view is sky-bound, too.

Bush elaborated on the inspirational spark of the song in a missive to her fan club newsletter in late 1985, reflecting, 'I used to do this a lot as a child, just watching the clouds go into different shapes. I think we forget these pleasures as adults . . . we feel silly about what we used to do naturally.' At the crossroads of past and future, Bush seems to be suggesting that the innocent pleasures of childhood are worth hanging on to; if you're not in a state of wonder at the universe around you, you might miss an important warning. As she put it, 'The song is also suggesting the coming of the next flood – how perhaps the "fools on the hills" will be the wise ones.'[9] In another interview that year, she spoke of her desire to hold on to childhood. 'Maybe bits of me don't want to grow up. Maybe I'm an escapist, a romantic. I dislike cynicism. It's bad energy. Does that make me childlike?'[10] 'Hounds of Love' evokes childhood memory, and 'The Big Sky' revels in innocent pleasures. The two remaining tracks on side A must contemplate the loss of that innocence, as children navigate complex transitions towards maturity.

'The Big Sky' was, according to guitarist David Rhodes, considered for inclusion in Bush's *Before The Dawn* concert residency in 2014. It was even rehearsed by the band once or twice.[11] Perhaps it was a wise decision to cut it from a show already so full of sky.

'Mother Stands for Comfort'

Shifting to A minor, 'Mother Stands for Comfort' ushers in a decidedly austere mood in the wake of the previous track's celebratory fade-out. Around a simple, rocking chair LinnDrum beat, Bush's expressive piano figures creep and wrap around dark, yearning chords. Contrasting against the simpler, more triadic approach to harmony writing heard on the album up to this point, this is the first composition on *Hounds Of Love* that bears the hallmarks of being written at the piano. The verse descends from Am7 to Fmaj9, then temporarily pauses on a hamstrung resolution of Am7 over an E bass. In the reciprocal phrase, it makes a hopeful move to D9 (suggesting dorian mode), then a melancholy pivot to B♭aug4/D, affecting a twisted phrygian modal cadence back to the tonic (Am7) to go around again. These chords are complicated by blurry dissonances and unstable non-root note footings. They move within the A minor tonal space as if searching for a way out. Bush's lead vocal traces the upper edges of the piano part, while Eberhard Weber's upright five-string electric bass provides a lower melodic counterpoint in warm, supple movements. The interaction is like an expressively choreographed duet, with Weber's malleable lines painting the lyric with emotional heaviness and also a distinct slipperiness. In this stark song world, the bassist's performance is the large, weary heart at the centre of the frame; it's constant and constantly bending.

The lyric is sung from the perspective of a guilty person, a self-confessed killer and liar, who understands that no matter what monstrous acts they commit their mother will always hide their wrongdoings and keep their secrets. Mum loves unconditionally and forgives all. As Bush explained, 'There are many different kinds of love and the track's really talking about the love of a mother, and in this case, she's the mother of a murderer, in that she's basically prepared to protect her son against anything.'[12] The warm, murmuring interior of the song is threatened by unquiet violence in the form of sudden loud tom hits, courtesy of Stuart Elliott, and the sharp sound of smashed glass, courtesy of the Fairlight.

The chorus introduces a cold, whistling Fairlight theme, naked and strange in the skeletal context of the arrangement. The beat is decorated with clanging, jagged impacts, processed with reverb and bitten by noise gates to resemble gunshots and the clatter of metallic pots and pans. The harmonies of the chorus cycle around a progression of minor chords – Am, Dm/F, Dm, Em7 – a bleak swirl that underpins the primary lyrical sentiment: 'Mother stands for comfort, mother will hide the murderer'. Bush's lead vocal performance is ambivalent, resigned, calm. By contrast, the backing vocals that enter ahead of the second chorus (at 1'43") are distilled primal emotion. High-pitched, wolf-like howls (*Ah-ooo! Ah-ooo-ah!*), an anguished squeal that sounds like a baby's scream (at 2'45") and, as the song draws to a close, agonized cries that echo, multiply and bleed through the stark sonic space.

'Mother Stands for Comfort' might feel like a diversion on side A, especially since it differs so dramatically in tone and mood to the tracks it sits between, not to mention it's the only track from this side that wasn't released as a single. However, it taps into a number of important themes seen throughout *Hounds Of Love*: the comfort of family, the primal nature of love and the fierceness of Mother Nature. It explores the unconditional nature of maternal love, which, far from being simply warm and cuddly, is more often made sharply manifest in the messiest moments of life. The business end of unconditional love, where there is zero ambiguity. On 'Jig of Life' we will see the lengths a mother will go to, transcending time and space, to protect her children's futures. This universal maternal urge, the animal instinct to protect and survive, can be cold and unsentimental as well as nurturing; that which is truly unbreakable must be made of tough stuff. 'Mother Stands for Comfort' is the downer that disturbs *Hounds Of Love*'s run of bangers, but it's also probably the deepest, psychologically heaviest cut on the record.

'Cloudbusting'

The final track on side A takes direct inspiration from one of the twentieth century's most controversial figures. Wilhelm Reich was a psychoanalyst, a colleague of Freud and Einstein. A liberationist who coined the term 'sexual revolution', he published a theory stating that frequent orgasms were the key to good health. He designed a device called the 'orgone accumulator', which he claimed would allow people to absorb the life force of the universe. Reich also developed another device at Orgonon, his home/laboratory in Maine, called the cloudbuster, which he claimed could manipulate the weather with this 'orgone energy'. His work led him to clash with the American authorities, and he was charged with fraud in 1956; he died of heart failure in prison the following year. But 'Cloudbusting' is not really about Reich, it's about the relationship he had with his son Peter, as remembered and understood from the boy's perspective.

Peter Reich published his autobiography, *A Book of Dreams*, in 1973. Nine years old when his father died, his writing explores fuzzy, melancholy childhood memories of life before and after that loss in impressionistic prose and dream imagery. Bush happened upon the volume in an occult bookshop in 1976. 'It was just calling me from the shelf, and when I read it I was very moved by the magic of it.'[13]

The first line of 'Cloudbusting' references Peter's memory-haunted dreams and continuing grief ('I still dream of Orgonon, I wake up crying'). Pulsing chamber strings, with something of the bite and edge of 'Winter' from Vivaldi's *Four Seasons*, establish an atmosphere of elegant excitement under the song's opening moments. They gently chop through a chord progression, the same harmonic formation that we heard in 'Running Up That Hill' (C natural minor, i - VII - VI), only now shifted up a step to the territory of C# minor: C#m down to B, then A, and back up again. Like 'Hounds of Love', this is another composition that has no need for bass or guitar. It's all strings, Fairlight and drums.

Live-played strings were performed by the Medici Quartet (extended to sextet size through the magic of studio overdubbing). Their parts were arranged for the ensemble by Dave Lawson, who had helped realize the string arrangement for 'Houdini' on *The Dreaming*. Aside from a brief moment when the sextet stretch out in curvaceous countermelody

during the second verse ('On top of the world' at 1'16"),
the group mostly remains focused on the obsessive staccato
bounce, in lockstep with a simple drum beat that places strict
emphasis on kick and snare.

Chorus sections are defined by an eager, step-wise
string melody that fidgets around a limited range. The
persistent repetition creates a growing tension that finds
a sudden release when Bush declares, 'Just saying it could
even make it happen' (2'27"), and the music breaks free
with a stirring Fairlight solo, all elbows and odd angles, a
fanfare that sounds at-once triumphant, sincere and naive.
From here, the soft, rain-like rumble of tom rhythms in
the background bursts into a heavy downpour of splashy,
layered marching snares. For the background singalong
(*yeah-ee-yeah-ee-yeah-eeee, yooo*), Bush layers up not only
her own voice but also the manly tones of Brian Bath, John
Carder Bush and Del Palmer. Paddy Bush's basso profundo
can also be heard harrumphing along with the bounding
pulse of the coda.

The cloudbuster sound that plays over the closing
moments was devised as a 'decoy effect' to mask the petering
out of the drums and strings. 'We covered the whole thing
over with the sound of a steam engine slowing down so that
you had the sense of the journey coming to an end . . . we
actually made up the sound effect out of various sounds,
and Del was the steam. And we got a whistle on the Fairlight
for the "poo poop".[14] The moment of 'arrival', symbolized by
Bush's steam train sound design, signifies a triumph over the
weather. Through faith and sheer force of will ('saying it can

even make it happen'), she – writing and singing as the child Peter Reich – has made it rain.

The lyric is peppered with troubling memories: having to bury a favourite toy, watching a parent forcibly taken away. Peter Reich, now a man, is haunted by memories of his dad ('Every time it rains, you're here in my head') and still clings to the feelings of magic that he felt as a child ('I just know that something good is going to happen'). The sad longing of the lyrics, combined with the hopeful, striving quality of the music, captures a poignant image. Loneliness, magic, grief. The bittersweet pain of growing up. '[The book is] so sad, but it's also got this beautiful kind of happy innocence that goes with childhood . . . [It] does get sadder as you can feel him hanging onto his childhood. The book really touched me, and the song is really trying to tell that story.'[15] The song's suitably cinematic extended video was conceived by Bush and Terry Gilliam and directed by Julian Doyle. Donald Sutherland plays Wilhelm, and Bush dresses in boyish drag to play the role of the young Peter. The mini-movie recreates the scene in the book when the father is arrested and his lab ransacked. As Wilhelm is driven away, Peter runs back to the cloudbuster and makes it rain all by himself.

Taken on its own, 'Cloudbusting' has a compelling narrative; it's one of those rabbit-hole songs that can lead listeners to the inspirational source text (*A Book of Dreams*) and further on to the wild world of Reich and his maverick research. But the song also functions meaningfully in the larger structure *Hounds Of Love*. It transports us to the world of dreams and nightmares. It is the arrival of the rain promised in the clouds of 'The Big Sky'. After successfully mastering the watery weather at the end of 'Cloudbusting', the tables are quickly turned when the listener flips the record over. In moments, Bush will be at the mercy of the elements, helplessly adrift in a drowning dream.

The Ninth Wave

A black-and-white portrait on the back cover, shot by John Carder Bush, depicts the artist floating on her back in a dark body of water. Weeds tangle in her hair and cling to the saturated fabric of her thin off-white dress. She is wearing a life jacket and reaching towards something we can't see. Her look is uncertain. This image shows Bush as the protagonist of *The Ninth Wave* and draws from romantic depictions of Pre-Raphaelite maidens adrift in water, such as John Everett Millais's 1852 painting of *Ophelia* in her nightdress, supine in a stream among the reeds, which inspired his contemporaries Arthur Hughes and John William Waterhouse's depictions of the *Lady of Shalott* (1873 and 1888, respectively). The Arthurian legend of Elaine of Astolat, aka the Lady of Shalott, a cursed woman who dies of heartbreak and whose final wish is to float past Camelot on an open boat, was popularized in an 1832 poem by Alfred, Lord Tennyson. Bush had referenced these poetic images in the special promo video for 'The Kick Inside' on a 1978 Dutch TV special filmed at Efteling amusement park,[1] where, dressed in mourning clothes and surrounded by flowers, she dies on a boat as it floats out onto a lake. On the album's back cover, these Pre-Raphaelite/

Arthurian references feel supported by a poetic verse quoted underneath Bush's watery, weed-strewn portrait, an excerpt from *The Coming of Arthur*, the first of Tennyson's 12-part cycle *Idylls of the King* (1859–85):

> *Wave after wave, each mightier than the last*
> *'Til last, a ninth one, gathering half the deep*
> *And full of voices, slowly rose and plunged*
> *Roaring, and all the wave was in a flame*

The lines describe the ocean during the thaumaturgical birth of King Arthur, who was plucked out of a raging sea by the wizard Merlin. As scholar Holly Kruse notes, 'the invocation of Arthur weaves a mythic web around the second side of *Hounds*'.[2] In 1930, occultist Dion Fortune wrote about possible Arthurian connections to the lost civilization of Atlantis, saying 'the songs of our own Keltic tradition [refer to] the lost land of Lyonesse, whose church bells can be heard ringing out in the Atlantic beyond the stormy coast of Cornwall where the dark figure of Merlin moves through the mist of legend'.[3] Images of drowned cities have appeared across Bush's work, from 'Atlantis' (1973), one of her earliest demos, to *Aerial*'s 'A Coral Room'. But wait, before we read too much into this, it turns out that *The Ninth Wave* wasn't inspired by Tennyson or Arthur after all, as 'actually it was the other way around', she explained. 'I wanted a title for the whole thing. I was looking through some books and found [the] quote.'[4]

No matter the original inspiration, the presentation on the back of the LP is a heady blend of references that evoke the magic and primeval power of the ocean: the force that destroys and the substance from which all things came to exist. In nautical folklore, it is believed that waves arrive in groups, the ninth being the largest and most destructive in the cycle. The ocean, as a metaphor for rebirth and enlightenment, is present not only in Tennyson's tale of Arthur but also in allegorical fiction such as Herman Melville's *Moby-Dick* and the psychological writings of Carl Jung, who identified the sea as 'the favourite symbol for the unconscious, the mother of all that lives'.[5] Bush said, 'I love the sea! It's the energy that's so attractive – the fact that it's so huge. And war films, where people would come off the ship and be stuck in the water with no sense of where they were or of time, like sensory deprivation. It's got to be ultimately terrifying.'[6]

The Ninth Wave is a connected suite of seven tracks that takes up all of side B. It details the experiences of a woman who is edging in and out of consciousness as she spends a night stranded in the ocean. With the little light on her lifejacket illuminating nothing but herself, the narrative makes use of exquisitely immersive composition and production techniques to render tactile her experiences of terror, isolation and catharsis. Do you want to feel how it feels?

'And Dream of Sheep'

The Ninth Wave begins in the same tonality of 'Cloudbusting', adrift in the dark waters of C# minor. The melody across the opening lines is marked by the distinctive upward interval of a perfect 5th; the words leap up from E to B ('Little light'), the vocal melody underlined by bright, ringing, piano octaves. The 5th is immediately restated ('shining'), from a lower B up to F#. These outstretched figures reach, with a sense of hopefulness, through the next lines ('Little light will guide them'), after which Bush turns the phrase back to herself with a C# minor resolution ('to me'). While the piano repeats the grasping figure in 5ths, the melody now remains focused around E ('My face is all lit up'). In the next phrase, Bush imagines what she might look like to a rescue party, chasing the 'white horses' of the curling waves, and as she sings, her voice clings to the top B of the first phrase, the image she is grasping towards. The hook of the song ('Let me be weak, let me sleep and dream of sheep') resolves with a gentle harmonic cadence. After the startling opening in what felt like C# minor, the closing phrase feels like being tucked into a warm, cosy bed in E major.

Throughout 'And Dream of Sheep' the upwards extension of the melody is the urgent blink of wakefulness; the sloping, softened melodies that curl downwards to tonal resolution are the figures that lull Bush's protagonist to the irresistible comfort of slumber. The opposing energies of these phrase shapes help illustrate the narrative ('If you fall asleep when you're in the water, I've heard that you roll over and so you drown, so they're trying to keep themselves awake'[7]) and engender an immersive atmosphere for the listener – the lullaby that both startles and soothes. The harmonic progressions waver between minor energy in the 'A' phrase, circling around the similar chord relationships of 'Cloudbusting' and 'Running Up That Hill', C#m7 to A6 then B (i - VI - bVII); in the 'B' phrase, the music feels comfortable and assured, with grounded harmonies that are vaguely familiar to what we've heard on 'Hounds of Love' and a similar pedal point tethering the emotion firmly in position: E (flashes of E6), F#m/E then B/E. The subtle use of these already established chord relationships from *Hounds Of Love* contributes to the soothing, subliminal magic of this track.

In the breaks between verses, we hear voices on the waves: a coastguard's radio transmission and the gentle voice of Bush's mother, Hannah, saying, 'come here with me now', something she had once said to her young daughter to comfort her after nightmares.[8] The arrangement is led by piano, and the texture is predominantly organic, with a brief flash of orchestration that swells dramatically through the words 'sound of engines', a crashing fortissimo C#m9 thrust that breaks and evaporates, weightless, across crashing waves and seagulls. Intimate touches of bouzouki (a lute-like instrument played by Dónal Lunny) and multitracked whistles (John Sheahan, affecting a folk-music approximation of the strange Fairlight sounds on side A) are tender and reassuring. Bush's vocal performance is delicate and dramatic, wrapped in arctic Quantec reverb; you can almost feel the chill mist on her breath.

A key detail is Bush admitting that being left with her anxious imagination is the most frightening part of the woman's predicament. She later explained, 'I find that horrific imagery, the thought of being completely alone in all this water . . . at the mercy of their imagination, which again I personally find such a terrifying thing, the power of one's own imagination being let loose on something like that.'[9] Across the final lines, as she follows her thoughts 'deeper and deeper' with a descending, wilted voice, the music stalls on the dominant

B7 over E – the song has no ending, but rather it connects directly to the nightmare hallucination of 'Under Ice'.

Twenty-nine years after the release of *Hounds Of Love*, Bush made a music video for the track, to be shown during the *Before The Dawn* shows in London. Floating in black waters, and wearing a lifejacket with a red light blinking, she sings the song live to an overhead camera. At the video's end, she slips under the water.

'Under Ice'

Heading down to the cold atmosphere of A minor, where 'Mother Stands for Comfort' also stood, the lean arrangement of 'Under Ice' consists of three layers of Fairlight (all using the TRAMCHLO preset that featured all over side A). One layer is a bass octave, poking rhythmically on the root notes; above it, a nervy staccato theme on parallel 5ths, and behind it, a Fairlight pad that holds an A (sus2) shape throughout.

The piece is through-composed, meaning that there are no repeating sections – the track is one continuous, unfolding movement from start to end. The synthetic staccato strings bring to mind the baroque flavours of 'Cloudbusting', connecting the sound to that song's themes of childhood memory and uneasy dreaming. Bush sings in sync with the parallel 5th Fairlight part, with accented rhythms in groups of three and two ('won-der-ful' . . . 'ev-'ry-where' . . . 'so-o' . . . 'whi-ite'). At the end of the phrase the music shifts pulse from 4/4 to 3/4 and back again. These changes to the metric pulse are irregular and not part of a pattern that can be anticipated, creating a sense of disorientation and strange displacement.

The lyrics say the song's setting is wonderful, but the music and sound design tell us different, with the bleak texture backdropped by the vague sounds of threatening wind and weather. Bush's voice is deep, tremulous and severe. Then a different voice – gentle, elongated, untethered from the stabbing Fairlight motif – describes the scene; a frozen river, no one else around, they're skating fast across the ice. By phrase end, the music switches metric footing (to 3/4) and voices converge in serrated rhythms and enunciated sibilance ('Splitting sound / silver heels spitting / spitting snow'). With mounting horror, Bush realizes the trapped figure moving under the ice is actually her. As she cries, 'It's meee! Ohh!', her voice reaches up high, only to slide slowly down as the pulse slackens to a stop, leaving the Fairlight pad shivering in the wind.

It is testament to Bush's production skills how vivid and frightening this frozen nightmare feels. Incidental sonic flourishes heighten the cinematic effect with indistinct distant voices, field recordings of waves, wind and thunder. Paddy Bush is credited for additional 'harmonic vocals' – the flickering overtones over the final drone, most likely sampled and manipulated in the Fairlight.

'Waking the Witch'

A sharp whisper ('Wake up!') and a surging backwards piano chord (C#(sus2)) drag us back to the watery, piano-led tonal zone of 'And Dream of Sheep'. Gentle suspended piano chords are refracted through a rhythmic delay, concentric circles of echo rippling from every touch. Voices speak from various locations in the stereo space, urging the woman to wake up; some of them sound like family ('Wake up, sleepy head!'), another like a scolding schoolmistress ('Wake up child – pay attention!'). The assemblage recalls the collage of answering machine farewells at the end of 'All the Love' from *The Dreaming*. Included in the sequence are voices from her immediate family, as well as Palmer, Brian Tench from the mixing team, even actor Robbie Coltrane. There is a flashback to 'And Dream of Sheep' ('Little light'), the sound of keening whale song and the foreshadowing of a moment soon to come as a crowd of background voices murmur lines from 'Jig of Life' and John Carder Bush's voice from the back of the right speaker peeks out to stage-whisper 'Over here!'

With the suggestion that the woman has a visitor ('Look who's here to see you!'), the track explodes into high alarm; a startled high piano tremolo rings out, an adrenal rhythm track kicks into motion with a jumpy, anxious drum pattern (Morgan doubling a LinnDrum sequence) and agitated muted guitar figures from Alan Murphy. Most shocking is Bush's frantic voice, cutting in and out as she pleads, 'Listen to me, help me, help me baby', her desperation rendered almost unintelligible, the garbled cries of a drowning person struggling to keep their head above water. The effect was achieved by quickly moving the record switch on the tape machine, an experiment that was apparently the source of a heated argument between Bush and Palmer. He later reflected in an interview with *Sound on Sound*. 'I said it would just be a mess, but she said, "Look, just do it, will you?" . . . of course it worked, and I had to eat humble pie. I've eaten so much humble pie over the years that I'm putting on weight!'[10]

Inside the nightmare, Bush plays multiple antagonistic roles, like the cast of inner accusers in 'Fullhouse' from *Lionheart* ('Imagination sets in, then all the voices begin'), as self-doubt and recrimination turn the woman's watery struggle for survival into a witch trial. She is the accused and also the interrogating Witchfinder, and she multiplies her voice to serve as the jury that condemns her. Witch 'swimming' or 'ducking' was the practice of tying up and dunking an accused woman into a body of water to see if they sank or floated; if they sank (and drowned), they were innocent. If they didn't, they were found guilty and executed.[11] Other tests included subjecting the accused to pain via burning and pricking, a practice based on the belief that witches bore a bloodless mark on their bodies that was impervious to pain. With its monstrous voice effect (Eventide Harmonizer set to minus-two octaves), Bush's Witchfinder subjects the accused to such tests ('You won't burn, you won't bleed, confess to me girl').

At the same time, background voices sing lines adapted from the halyard sea shanty *Blood Red Roses*. The tune was popularized by folk revivalist A. L. (Bert) Lloyd. Lloyd appeared, uncredited, leading the song in John Huston's 1956 film *Moby Dick*. The chorus of *Blood Red Roses* ('Oh, you pinks and posies, go down you blood red roses, go down!') is said by some folklorists to refer to the gore of a harpooned whale. Here, Bush riffs on Lloyd in the lines, 'Pinks and posies, red, red roses, go down'. Even though we don't have room in this book to explore the B-sides from *Hounds Of Love*, it's worth mentioning that the title track, released as the third single, had a cover of Lloyd and Ewan MacColl's 'The Handsome Cabin Boy' on the B-side; another sea shanty, this one is about a mischievous girl who disguises herself as a boy to gain employment on a ship. By the end of the song, she has fallen pregnant to the captain and is lusted after by his wife. It's a humorous ditty that sits well in proximity to the transgressive gender fantasies of 'Running Up That Hill', the sea-bound setting of *The Ninth Wave* and the evocation of Lloyd and the threat of the female in 'Waking the Witch'.

The music breaks away from C# minor for a counter phrase that swirls with the sound of church bells and woozy spiralling guitar figures around E minor. Bush murmurs snatches of Catholic Vulgate scripture that she may be forgetting or getting wrong: 'Spiritus sanctus in nomine no-no-no-no' (*the name of the Holy Spirit, no*) and later 'Deus et dei domino no-no-no-no'[12] (*God and God's lord, no*). When the music returns to the C# minor riff, prickly synth sequences by Kevin McAlea and Fairlight bass programmed by Palmer escalate the drama as Bush offers her confession in a stuttering, distorted voice. The Witchfinder questions her innocence and a jury proclaims her guilt, the verdict hammered home by onerous tribal drums. She cries out, 'Help this blackbird / There's a stone around my leg'. As the Witchfinder growls and groans in fury, about to seal her fate, the nightmare spell is broken by the sound of a rescue helicopter and a voice shouting, 'Get out of the waves, get out of the water'. The helicopter sound effect was the same sample that was used on Pink Floyd's *The Wall* (1979).

The blackbird in the lyric could be a reference to Elizabeth George Speare's 1958 novel *The Witch of Blackbird Pond*, where the main character is seen as suspicious after diving into the ocean to retrieve a child's doll; her ability to swim – and, later, read and teach others how to read – leads her to being accused of witchcraft. Bush described the track as touching on wider issues such as 'the fear of women's power', adding, 'I feel that female intuition and instincts are very strong, and are still put down.'[13] The combined effect of jarring, stop-start rhythms, altered voices, the accumulated aura of unsettling references (whaling shanties, Catholic prayer and confession, horrific witch trials, *The Wall*, *Moby-Dick* and *The Witch of Blackbird Pond*) make 'Waking the Witch' a harrowing listening experience. Years later, Bush admitted to feeling disappointed with how her Eventide Harmonizer-enhanced performance as the Witchfinder turned out, saying, 'I think if I had more energy, I would've pursued that with an actor doing the speaking part rather than myself.'[14] Personally, I love Bush's performance, as it highlights the presence of an accusatory Jungian shadow within the nightmare sequence. I feel it also resonates with the similar transformative effect heard over the closing moments of 'Running Up That Hill', creating a tissue of connection between these songs that explore the dis/empowering aspects of gender.

'Watching You Without Me'

As shuddering chopper blades fade into the distance, 'Watching You Without Me' blinks awake in a different realm.

An uncannily calm and empty atmosphere is measured by a minimal LinnDrum rhythm, augmented with side-stick backbeat and a syncopated floor tom by Stuart Elliott. Bush's voice mumbles a quick oscillation across a 5th, sounding like a car engine that won't start – a trapped utterance glitching between repelling magnetic fields. The Fairlight figures that enter are also stretched, not only across the intervallic 5th but also the extreme stereo space. The music rocks back and forth between B♭ and C (the same chord relationship, ♭VII to I, of 'The Big Sky') like a hypnotist's swinging watch. Danny Thompson's rubbery double bass gurns and twists in sympathetic counterpoint to Bush's frustrated moans. Elliott's playing ticks along with strict precision, evoking the metronomic second hand of a clock, with a pulse that cleverly hangs just slightly below sixty beats per minute. Mumble-mouthed backing vocals sing, 'You can't hear me . . . you can't hear what I'm saying'. Before the main vocal starts, the song has already set the scene atmospherically – we are in a liminal space between life and death, wakefulness and sleep; Bush is trapped in limbo.

The verse sets out the altered context, as the woman observes her loved ones back at home, waiting with growing concern for her return. 'They're at home, in spirit, seeing their loved one sitting there waiting for them . . . But there's no way that you can actually communicate, because they can't see you.'[15] Despite its strangely dulcet atmosphere, the song is 'more of a nightmare than anything so far', she explained to her fan club, 'because this is the closest she's been to any kind of comfort, and yet it's the furthest away'.[16]

Shapely swells of string orchestra (arranged by Michael Kamen) surge and recede around key words – 'I'm not *here*', 'There's a *ghost* in our *home*' – and pepper the rhythmic texture of the second verse with light pizzicato. With the soft whine of radio static and a morse code 'SOS' message, the song bursts out of its trance at 2'19" to a bright Hindustani teental rhythm, complete with hand cymbals (a rare exception to *Hounds Of Love*'s no-cymbals rule) and even a little vocal 'yip' worked into the loop. The lead vocal ('Don't ignore, don't ignore me') is sung backwards, double-tracked at the octave; a snaking melodic movement that is matched by Kamen's voluptuous tutti strings. This moment recalls two experiments from *The Dreaming*: the backwards singing on 'Leave it Open' and the spoken South Indian taal rhythm (*konnakol*) across the coda of 'Get Out of My House' (performed by Esmail Sheikh). In keeping with the theme of blocked communication, not all of the backwards vocals are clearly legible, particularly towards the end of the section at 2'48" when Bush might be singing the words 'we really see' (or possibly 'releasing') across an upwards-spiralling melisma. If you reverse the audio in this section, it sounds like she is singing 'be silly' over and over. Then, a series of shocks, and the chopped vocal of 'Waking the Witch' returns with a desperate plea for help ('Listen to me, help me baby, talk to me'). The horror of communication failure between ghost realms and reality has been a rich theme in Bush's work ('Wuthering Heights', 'Houdini'), and in 'Watching You Without Me' she lets you *feel* the frustration and loneliness of insurmountable distance.

'Jig of Life'

The starting point for 'Jig of Life' took inspiration from the ceremonial music of the Anastenaria, a centuries-old ecstatic dance and fire-walking ritual performed during religious feasts in Greece and Bulgaria. The music, inspired by a rare recording that Paddy Bush had found and shared with his sister, is characterized by repetitious, deep, rolling rhythms and whirling figures performed on violin and tsabouna (Greek bagpipe). Bush said she was drawn to it because 'people worked themselves into a trance state through the hypnotic quality of the music'[17] and she lifted the musical and rhythmic elements of the style, which we hear across the first section of the song. Based on the Greek dhrómi mode (on a root of A), the tonality is mostly minor but with idiomatic instability on the second degree (B), throwing up an occasional B♭ in the swirling flow of melody and hitting wonderfully dissonant pinch points at 0'44" and 1'33".

In the lyric, Bush greets an image of her future self ('Hello, old lady'), who has made a timely visit to ensure that she doesn't give up in her fight to survive ('Let me live, girl'). The temporal urgency of the message is underlined in Bush's solemn delivery as the old lady explains that it's not only her future that depends on Bush surviving the present, but the lives of her yet-unborn children. Within the musical churn of ecstatic folk-music, the mention of 'the place where the crossroads meet' evokes once again the image of Hecate, the goddess in Greek mythology who is often depicted flanked by two dogs and sometimes shown with a triple-formed face that sees the past, present and future simultaneously.

'Jig of Life' doesn't just draw from Greek folklore. Bush also taps the traditional music of her own maternal ancestors. The 'B' section at 1'40" shifts to an instrumental break built around Celtic folk melody. Beginning on John Sheahan's fiddle with a deft melodic turn that flips between A major and A dorian, the music intensifies to a boisterous jig that's thrillingly physical and full of blood. This moment, arranged by Bill Whelan, is a showcase for the Irish musicians that Bush had travelled to Dublin to capture: Sheahan on fiddle, Dónal Lunny on bouzouki and bodhran, and Liam O'Flynn on uillean pipes.

The jig stops dead and Bush repeats to herself, 'I put this moment . . . here'. Her words are separated across the extreme width of the stereo field at first, moving closer towards a possible connection when John Carder Bush's voice interrupts with 'Over here!' and the opening ceremonial theme strikes up once again. He delivers a rousing performance of his own poetic verse, speaking on the convergence of 'when', 'then' and 'now' riding in on the waves, the ocean as the primordial force transforming the 'laughing girl' into a 'woman unfurled'. Curiously, a fan who spoke with him relayed a story that the poem was originally intended for an Irish performer to read, but it was decided to have him adopt an Irish accent to read it, with the intent of pitching the voice up to a female register (presumably with the same Eventide Harmonizer technology used on 'Running Up That Hill' and 'Waking the Witch').[18] It's easy to imagine how utterly mad that would have sounded, and it's no surprise the notion was abandoned; however, the poem and its function within the song would certainly hit differently if it was delivered in the feminine voice. Still, it remains a wonderfully generous and loving juncture in the context of *The Ninth Wave*. A magical and affirming moment of temporal self-care; the powers of mothers from the past and future rallying at the crisis point to help Bush choose to live.

'Hello Earth'

With 'The Big Sky' functioning as a structural stitch in the narrative of *Hounds Of Love*, so too 'Hello Earth' gathers together the musical, sonic and lyrical themes of the album into a single focal point at the climax of *The Ninth Wave*. Running at a little more than six minutes, it's the longest track on the album. It also has the most players, with drummer Stuart Elliott, guitarist Brian Bath, bassist Eberhard Weber, pipes by O'Flynn and bouzouki by Lunny, in addition to a choir (the Richard Hickox Singers), orchestral strings, horns and percussion, arranged again by Kamen. 'Hello Earth' is *big*, like symphonic-big, high-drama Hollywood-big. And like 'The Big Sky', it was a challenge to finish. '[It] was a very difficult track to write . . . in some ways it was too big for me.'[19] The problem was structural; Bush couldn't come up with a chorus that had the appropriate atmosphere and gravitas that the track demanded.

The lyric turns the ocean into a mirror, with our protagonist now looking down on earth from outer space. She notes the planet's insignificance in the universal scheme of things ('With just one hand . . . I can blot you out') borrowing imagery from Neil Armstrong's observation from space: 'I put up my thumb and shut one eye, and my thumb blotted out the planet Earth.'[20] She is helpless to stop a destructive storm she sees forming over America and moving out to sea ('Can't do anything . . . '). Bush calls back to 'Hounds of Love' (the declarative 'Here I go, don't let me go!' becomes a regretful 'Why did I go?'), 'Waking the Witch' ('Get out of the waves, get out of the water'), with keyword nods to 'Mother Stands for Comfort' ('Murderer!') and 'Cloudbusting' ('Out of the cloudburst'). The music returns to *The Ninth Wave*'s oceanic home in C# minor and the motivic chord progressions of 'And Dream of Sheep', 'Cloudbusting' and 'Running Up That Hill'. At sections beginning at 0'58" and 3'03", the music calls back to the chorus of 'Running Up That Hill'. Like a song in a Broadway musical that folds in all the show's themes into one piece, these restatements bring the forces of everything that has gone before to the surface of the narrative. The construction is satisfyingly handled, and the puzzle pieces fit together. The only problem was the large gaps ('huge, great holes') where the choruses should be. 'I'd had this idea to put a vocal piece in there . . . this traditional tune I'd heard used in [Werner Herzog's 1979 film] *Nosferatu* [*the Vampyre*]. And everything I came up with, it was rubbish really, compared to what this piece was saying.'

British composer Michael Berkeley was tasked with transcribing and arranging a version of the Georgian folk song 'Zinzkaro' (trans. 'By the Spring') for an ensemble of male members of the Richard Hickox Singers. The arrangement needed to be similar to the haunting version featured in Herzog's film, but also tailored to fit within the existing gaps of 'Hello Earth'. Conservatoire-trained, Berkeley characterized Bush's creative approach as 'zany [and] ambitious', later recalling how he was sent a cassette with copious colourful notes, adding, 'she talked of the sound quality in the most graphic terms . . . indeed, she was thrilled when I suggested we create our own new language for this chorus of the spheres'.[21] The version of 'Zinzkaro' heard in *Nosferatu* is in F mixolydian, and this tonality was retained for the 'Hello Earth' arrangement, with its relationship to the rest of the song in C# minor 'arriving as something foreign, harmonically a surprise, as though from another world'. The movement from the solemn ambience of the choral section as it slides back the verse, with the lowest strings oozing down from F to C# and the highest strings inching upwards from high C to C#, is a spine-tingling musical manoeuvre, a panoramic aspect ratio shift.

'Hello Earth' peaks with intensity at its mid-point; from 3'25" the 'Zinzkaro' theme repeats three times, above an F drone, solemn and still. At around 5'30", a final, queasy, slow-motion portamento slides outwards to a chilly, widescreen drone on C#. Snatches of whale song and soft sonar blips suggest a sinking into oceanic depths as Bush whispers in German, '*Tiefer, tiefer, irgendwo in der tiefe gibt es ein licht*' (trans. 'Deeper, deeper, somewhere in the depths there is a light'). This final descent could be interpreted as the moment of death for our struggling heroine or a crucial moment of psychological reckoning in the dark night of the soul, the Jungian 'night sea journey' that 'descends into the dark, hot depths of the unconscious'.[22] The pull 'deeper and deeper' fulfils the promise of 'And Dream of Sheep', with Bush finally soothing the 'little earth' to sleep after her long struggle to stay alert. The last voice we hear is that of a whale, bringing to mind *Moby-Dick*, another archetypal night sea journey of darkness and psychological transformation.

'The Morning Fog'

As the edges of the world come back into focus in the morning light, the final track of *The Ninth Wave* concludes the suite with lightness. While the lyrics remain ambiguous about whether Bush gets rescued, the music is reassuringly bright in B major, bobbing down from B to Asus2 and E/G# and back up again without a hint of darkness or danger. John Williams's double-tracked nylon string guitar decorates the gently pulsing LinnDrum sequence with delicate picked rhythms and improvised melody overflowing in sunlit sweetness. Palmer's fretless bass is wonderfully buoyant and playful. As Bush sings 'The light . . . begin to breathe', background voices interject in spirited shanty-style call and response with Irish folk-style *diddling* ('*Do dum dee-a dum doo*').

Bush sings about falling 'like a stone, like a storm', which could suggest to some that she is being pulled down into the water's depths one last time, or alternatively that she is falling to earth with gravity, back to safety. Her feeling of being 'born again into the sweet morning fog' is a transforming rebirth; alive or not, she emerges into the light on the other side of the ordeal, understanding herself and how to love and appreciate others in a better way. After all of the communication issues that plagued Bush throughout *Hounds Of Love* and *The*

Ninth Wave, she is now able to tell her loved ones honestly, and with a full heart of enlightened appreciation, how she feels ('D'you know what? I love you better now'). The whole of *Hounds Of Love* has been a journey towards learning how to love and here is the point of arrival, catharsis and closure.

'It's very much a song of seeing perspective, of being so grateful for everything that you have', Bush explained, adding, 'it was also meant to be one of those "thank you and goodnight" songs. You know, the little finale where everyone does a little dance and then the bow and then they leave the stage.'[23] Like a curtain call, Bush takes a moment to namecheck the members of her family unit in the final moments of the song: her mother, father, partner and brothers. And with that, the song takes a small bow, resolving with a dainty falling 5th on Williams's classical guitar.

Someone Lost at Sea Hoping to be Found by Someone in the Big Sky

The simple image at the heart of *The Ninth Wave*, a woman lost at sea, is one that has resurfaced in Bush's work over the years. The flashing red light of a life jacket, symbolic of a faint but sustaining hope, appeared again in an original artwork made by Bush that she donated to an auction in aid of the War Child charity in 1994. The works were a pair of almost-matching pieces; two small rectangles of black velvet set inside black and gold frames, each with a small flashing red light. The only difference between them is the text etched into the gold title plate affixed at the bottom. One says, 'Someone

Lost at Sea Hoping Someone in a Plane Will Find Them', the other, 'Someone in a Plane Hoping to Find Someone Lost at Sea'. The simple, mirrored design is an obvious reference to *The Ninth Wave* and its message of hope and survival in the midst of isolation and darkness. It's an image that only grows more resonant and meaningful as the decades roll by.

In late 2023, Bush revisited the concept with 'The Boxes of Lost at Sea', a special presentation of *Hounds Of Love* reissued on vinyl. The two wall-mountable boxes, each holding one side of the album, show a small, blinking red light set within a triangle-shaped depression, lined in black felt. Like the War Child pieces, the boxes feature gold plaques, now revised to highlight the mirrored perspectives between sides A and B of *Hounds Of Love*. From side A, looking down ('Someone in the Big Sky Hoping to Find Someone Lost at Sea') and from side B, looking up ('Someone Lost at Sea Hoping to be Found by Someone in the Big Sky').

Around the time of the release of *Hounds Of Love* in 1985, Bush spoke about her wish to turn side B into a film ('*The Ninth Wave* was written very much as a story, and ideally I would like to make a film of that'[24]). In her 2005 *Mojo* interview, she referred to the song cycle as 'my first novelette . . . I thought it was the beginning of something really interesting. It's just the idea of taking a piece of music on a journey.'[25] *The Ninth Wave* would indeed become something of a film, with dramatic scenes and live-sung performances shot in a deep-water tank at Pinewood Studios, just outside London, that were destined to be embedded into Act 2 of the lavish music-theatrical *Before The Dawn* shows in 2014. A journey from aural to visual realization that took twenty-nine years.

A ritual in six steps

Step one: 'Lily'

Begin with a prayer. Lily Cornford will recite the ancient *Gāyātri* mantra, a Sanskrit hymn, for you:

> *O thou who givest sustenance to the universe, from whom all things proceed, to whom all things return, unveil to us the face of the true spiritual sun, hidden by a disc of golden light, that we may know the truth and do our whole duty as we journey to thy sacred feet.*

Then, cast a circle of fire and summon the guardians. The Golden Dawn's Lesser Banishing Ritual of the Pentagram will evoke the presence of protecting angels at four cardinal points: Raphael of the air (to the east), Gabriel of water (west), Michael of fire (south) and Uriel of the earth (north). In *Before The Dawn*, the angels are positioned differently; Gabriel is now before you. On the path to becoming aerial, you must first pass through the water, westward towards the setting sun.

Step two: 'Hounds of Love', 'Joanni'

Summon your courage. Say to yourself: 'Here I go! / Don't let me go / Never let me go / Tie me to the mast!' Behold a vision of Saint Joan of Arc, the archetypal image of courage and faith. Angels speak to her with voices of fire ('les voix du feu') carried on the bells of Rouen.

Step three: 'Top of the City', 'Running Up That Hill', 'King of the Mountain'

Raise your power. Climb up on the angel's shoulders, run up that building, higher and higher, right over the top. Sing loudly, bang the drum, feel the storm rising. Le Prestidigitateur (the conjuror, *Before The Dawn*'s percussionist Mino Cinélu) will wield the sacred bullroarer to summon a tempest: a mighty wave that gathers half the deep, roaring and full of voices, all the wave in a flame.

Step four: 'The Ninth Wave'

Survive the witch trial and survive the night 'til the light begins to breathe, begins to speak . . .

Step five: 'A Sky of Honey'

As the dawn comes in with the golden light, can you hear the birdsong? The mistle thrush and the wood pigeon, the chaffinch and the robin, the blackbird and the siskin? Golden light dripping? And a golden bell? Ring it! Shake it down! Bring it on! Let it in! *Ding dong ding dong ding dong ding dong.* And when your beautiful wings are ready to fly, get up on that roof. High up on the roof, in the sun.

Step six: 'Among Angels', 'Cloudbusting'

Close the circle. Don't forget to acknowledge the angels and their help, it's only polite. Now you're on top of the world, looking over the edge.

Before The Dawn

> At the time of the release of *Hounds of Love* I had
> written a sketch of a script for 'Ninth Wave' ... but we
> just couldn't get it off the ground. In many ways it
> lends itself better to the medium of stage.
> – Kate Bush, *Before The Dawn* programme, 2014

On 14 May 1979, after an exhausting run of dates that took
her around the UK and Europe, Kate Bush finished her first
tour at the Hammersmith Odeon. Far from the average late
1970s travelling rock show, *Tour of Life* was a full-blown
music-theatrical extravaganza with mime, magic, burlesque,
dance, costume changes, projections and props. It had a rigid
set list that left no room for chat, no slipping of the mask.
Melody Maker proclaimed it 'the most significant spectacle
ever encountered in the world of rock'. It set a high watermark
for theatrical pop shows, topping even Bowie's *Diamond
Dogs Tour* with its level of vaudevillian camp. It anticipated
an important step change in pop performance – projected
visuals, group choreography and the first appearance of
head-mics (all of these became the norm for 1980s gigs).

Reviewers buzzed about what wild things Bush might do next. No one anticipated 'next' would take thirty-five years.

As the decades rolled by, Bush's fans came to terms with her absence from the stage. Her hard-won non-touring arrangement with EMI meant they couldn't compel her to hit the road. Like The Beatles from 1966 onwards, Bush chose to focus her creative energies in the recording studio. But the theatrical impetus of her artistry never went away. In 1985, she spoke about turning *The Ninth Wave* into a film. 'I love the idea of combining music and visuals. I think they are parallel entities.'[1] When asked if she would play *Hounds Of Love* live, she kicked the idea further down the road, saying that first she wanted to 'get into the visual thing on *The Ninth Wave*, and then I can maybe think about live work'.[2] That plan would end up on the backburner, and many assumed the project was abandoned. But what she said turned out to be true; returning to 'the visual thing' she had in mind for *The Ninth Wave* became the starting point for what brought her back to the stage.

The announcement of concert residency *Before The Dawn* on 21 March, 2014, caught everyone off guard. Bush and her collaborators (referred to as The KT Fellowship) had kept the project a tight secret for more than a year. The original plan for fifteen performances was stretched to twenty-two after the presale allocation failed to meet the demand. The shows went on general sale at 9.30 am on 28 March – all of the tickets were sold by 9.45.

She could have done a short run in an arena with nothing more than a piano and a microphone and nobody would have been disappointed. But what Bush had in mind was the most ambitious undertaking of her career. Bertie, fifteen-year-old Albert McIntosh, was instrumental in bringing *Before The Dawn* to life. She said, 'Without my son Bertie, this would never have happened. Without his encouragement and enthusiasm, particularly in the early stages when I was very frightened and afraid to push the "go" button, I'm sure I would have backed out.'[3] It would, as per the plan, incorporate film and theatrical staging. In development, the show began to assume a synchronous magic:

> One thing I hadn't accounted for was that 'it', the project itself, had a very strong opinion . . . [for] 'Watching You Without Me' I liked the idea of a short scene of dialogue. I immediately thought of David Mitchell, the author. He leapt into my mind but then I lost the nerve. A few days later I received an email from him . . . 'it' wanted him.
>
> – *Before The Dawn* programme

These synchronicities led to more chance encounters with choice collaborators who just happened to be free: musical director Nick Skilbeck, co-director Adrian Noble, set designer Dick Bird. Musicians were chosen for their skill and sensitivity: drummer Omar Hakim (Weather Report, Bowie) and percussionist Mino Cinélu (also Weather Report, Miles Davis), the show's beating hearts; bassist John Giblin (Peter Gabriel), multi-instrumentalist Jon Carin (Pink Floyd), guitarists David Rhodes (Gabriel again) and Friðrik Karlsson, and from *Tour of Life*, Kevin McAlea, on keyboards, accordion and uilleann pipes. The chorus players were plucked from London's theatre scene: Jacqui DuBois, Jo Servi, Sandra Marvin and Bob Harms, joined by Bertie, to sing background and act/dance. The venue needed to be small-to-medium-sized, able to host surround sound, mobile lighting, set pieces and flying backdrops. The dilapidated Eventim Apollo (formerly Hammersmith Odeon), the last stage she performed on in 1979, was chosen – it underwent renovations in 2013 that allowed The Fellowship time to set everything up to her exacting specifications. With seating for 3,632, it was intimate enough for the audience to see and take note of the carefully embedded details – with Bush, we know the goddess is always in the details – but just as important, she would be able to see and sense the crowd, too.

Whenever Bush was pressed on her reluctance to perform, she was open about being shy. In a 1985 interview for *Musician*, when Peter Swales brought up the plight of American fans who had been 'deprived' of seeing her live, Bush explained that her absence from the stage was a confidence issue, saying, 'If I can be the character in the song, then suddenly there's all this strength and energy in me which perhaps I wouldn't normally have, whereas if it was just me, I don't think I could walk on the stage with confidence.'[4] More than three decades later, while promoting the live album of *Before The Dawn* on the BBC, Bush made repeated reference to her performance anxiety. The key word was *terrified*: 'Were you quite nervous?' 'Yeah, I was terrified' (3'06"); 'I was terrified of doing live work as a performer again' (3'25"); 'I was so terrified that if my mind wandered off, that when I came back I wouldn't remember where I was' (13'22"); 'Before I went on? Absolutely terrified' (33'57"). The most challenging aspect was the first act, which wasn't covered by a theatrical presentation:

I knew that I wanted to start with 'Lily', because the whole thing starts with a prayer. And I very much wanted this involvement of everybody in the theatre, being part of this prayer that would protect us all through the journey that we were all going to go on . . . I found that the hardest part of the show to perform, that first set, because, you know, there was nowhere to hide.

– Kate Bush, BBC interview, 2016[5]

Act 1

And so it begins with a prayer, the recorded voice of Lily Cornford, reciting a version of the *Gāyātri* mantra. As the hypnotic, sidewinding groove of 'Lily' snakes across an extended introduction, anticipation in the venue becomes almost unbearable. Finally, she appears, looking radiant, dressed in black and barefoot, leading a procession of backing singers. As she sings, 'Oh Lily, I'm so afraid, I fear I am walking in the VEIL OF DARKNESS!', her voice splits into multiple cavernous echoes. It is the earthier, revised version from *Director's Cut* (2011), and she growls through new lyrics in the coda, including the audience in her protecting ritual: 'The hunter! A hunter! Put your angels up/ Put them all around us'. Then the hunt is on. Bertie starts the familiar cry, 'It's in the trees! It's coming!'. 'Hounds of Love' generates a great rush of emotion in the room; Bush proclaims, 'Well, here I go!', later gesturing to the crowd with 'Help me, help me please, I need love'. Listening to the live album, you can get a sense of what it was like to be there, party to a direct exchange of love and honesty between artist and audience. Everyone was so thankful to have her back. And she needed us to help her get through what was to come.

Armed with love and now ensconced within a circle of protection, the band kicks into 'Joanni' (*Aerial*, 2005), introducing one of the recurring themes of *Before The Dawn*: the tolling bells from Rouen Cathedral (a field recording made by McAlea on Joan of Arc Day, they were triggered on his keyboard). It is an evocation of Saint Joan, whose courageous statement, 'I am not afraid, for God is with me. I was born to do this', ties in with themes of protection, empowerment and overcoming one's fears at the top of the show. Joan was tried as a witch, but was never proven to be a heretic. Instead, she was charged with cross-dressing, an image of gender transgression that softly resonates with the lyrical themes of 'Running Up That Hill', 'Waking The Witch', 'Somewhere in Between' (*Aerial*) and the lyrical pun of being mistaken for a buoy in 'And Dream of Sheep'.

Any doubts over whether Bush still had the vocal chops to sing live are obliterated by the time 'Top of the City' (*The Red Shoes*, but here closer to the version from *Director's Cut*) reaches its explosive chorus. When the familiar ghostly drone of 'Running Up That Hill' fades in, the energy in the room, already electric, shifts up several gears. The momentum continues upwards, ascending with 'King of the Mountain' (*Aerial*), its whistling wind growing increasingly turbulent, led by tempestuous, virtuoso drumming from Hakim and Bush's increasingly frantic warnings of 'a storm rising!' In the live album's liner notes, Bush explains how percussionist Cinélu conjured the inclement weather. 'We called him Le Prestidigitateur. In the closing bars of "King of the Mountain" he commanded the front of the stage with the bullroarer, a sacred Aboriginal instrument which is traditionally forbidden to be heard by women . . . This was the moment when Mino summoned a great storm that pulled everyone on stage into *The Ninth Wave*.' At the height of the storm comes a mighty crash and small strips of yellow tissue paper rain down, upon which the relevant verse from *The Coming of Arthur* is written in the style of Tennyson's own hand, marking the transition to the narrative zone of *The Ninth Wave*.

Act 2

The second act begins with a brief filmed interlude, 'The Astronomer's Tale'. The astronomer (played by Kevin Doyle, known for his roles in *Downton Abbey* and *Happy Valley*) is watching a meteor shower when he receives a message of distress from a ship called Celtic Deep. The scene lasts just long enough for the stage to be reset, and when the curtain is raised, the band is repositioned at the back of the stage. Dick Bird's vast 'wreck wave' set wraps around the space, looking like the outer remains of a sunken ship, and also a bit like a whale's ribcage.

Regarding how the filmed components of *The Ninth Wave* would work alongside live staging, Bush explained in the programme: 'One of the very first ideas was to mix film with stage work and I thought it could be interesting if the real events took place on the screen in the form of pre-filmed footage and the nightmares and delirium took place live on stage. Hopefully achieving a sense of filmic crossfades between the two.' In the blackness, an oval screen flickers to life for 'And Dream of Sheep', showing the pre-filmed performance from the water tank at Pinewood Studios. The chill in her voice was authentic; she contracted a mild case of hypothermia during the shoot. As her body sinks into black water, the stage comes to life, drenched in deep indigo light, billowing eddies of fabric moving across the stage floor. Pacing menacingly about the space are two walking fish skeletons (dubbed 'Lords of the Waves' in the programme). Entering the nightmare world for 'Under Ice', Bush performs slow-motion skating movements in sync with the chorus behind her. At the horrific realization that she is the one trapped under the ice ('it's meeee ohh!'), Bush is dragged backwards into darkness by the Lords, while the chorus attacks the ground with pickaxes and chainsaws, opening a trap door and, in a clever bit of *The Prestige*-style misdirection, pull Bush's limp body out of the hole.

As her sleeping body resurfaces on the screen, voices from 'Waking the Witch' speak from all corners of the theatre's multi-channel surround system, begging the woman to wake up. Kicking in with a flurry of strobing lights in the dream space, Bush is delivered to the feet of the Witchfinder (Jo Servi). With the opposing vocal parts coming from two people, the original idea behind Bush's vocals from 1985 is better understood; the deep groans and grunts I once heard as the salacious excitement of the 'Witchfinder' are now clearly coming from the lost woman; her voice momentarily turns monstrous, evoking something of Mercedes McCambridge's performance as *The Exorcist*'s demon. Mimicking a ducking trial, the chorus pushes her down the trapdoor. A mobile lighting rig becomes a helicopter that moves over the crowd, shining searchlights at the trapdoor, momentarily capturing a glimpse of Bush re-emerging, flapping blackbird wings. The helicopter lurches over the audience, casting a bright searchlight around the venue. A radio transmission from the operator (voiced by Paddy Bush) explains that all passengers of the Celtic Deep have been rescued, bar a single 'missing female'.

After such high drama, light relief arrives by way of a short skit, 'Watching Them Without Her'. Bertie and actor Bob Harms play the lost woman's son and husband in a domestic scene. The pair engage in gentle banter over a burnt dinner and the football, sitting on a couch within a tilted, skew-whiff, floating room that bobs and slides back and forth on the ocean floor. An apparition of the drowning woman haunts the scene and sings 'Watching You Without Me', affecting *Poltergeist*-style electrical disturbances as she attempts to communicate with her family through the veil. From the darkness, Bertie's voice shouts 'Mum!', which jolts the woman on the screen awake. She cries out in anguish ('Let me live!') as the chorus performs a brief, new composition, 'Little Light'. Little more than a segue, the music wraps the motivic theme from 'And Dream of Sheep' around solemn, knotty vocal harmonies and stirring piano figures.

During 'Jig of Life', the skeletal Lords appear with billowing sheets that catch the air like huge kites; they move in sequence across the stage in successions of rolling waves, upon which are projected images of green ocean swirls and white horses. On the screen, Bush brings her hands to her chest, saying, 'I put this moment . . . here', while on stage a frozen television pops out of the ground with John Carder Bush reciting the poem that ends the song ('over here').

The staging of 'Hello Earth' removes much of the ambiguity of *The Ninth Wave*'s conclusion. In another pre-filmed clip from the chilly Pinewood tank, Bush sings the verse in water brilliantly illuminated by a halo of reflected moonlight. With the words 'I get out of my car' she grasps the edge of a buoy while, in the dream, a gigantic buoy also appears, glowing with bright red light and floating on an ocean of reflected stars. Members of the chorus ride upon it, holding red flares aloft as they sing the mournful Georgian chorale 'Zinzkaro'. The Lords detach Bush's seemingly lifeless body from the buoy, slowly carrying her off the stage and down the venue's aisle in a sombre funereal procession. Suddenly on the screen a hand reaches down, another hand grasps back, and halfway down the aisle, Bush stirs. Gathering at the front of the stage, now bathed in the warm light of dawn, the whole company joins in with an acoustic rendition of 'The Morning Fog'. Now unmasked, the Lords hoist their fish heads onto their shoulders and dance gracefully with the members of the chorus. Bush walks back through the venue and on to the stage to gigantic cheers. Singing the line 'D'you know what? I love you better now', she gestures to the crowd and smiles. The audience mirror back the very same sentiment with waves of rapturous applause.

Act 3

In tone and content, *A Sky of Honey* feels like the complementary opposite of *The Ninth Wave*. Where one narrative is the struggle to survive a dark and dangerous night, the other concerns the passing of an extremely pleasant summer's day. Both manifest transformation – first, the self-knowledge gained from enduring a challenging experience, and second, the experience of ecstasy and transcendence in the natural world. Bush's original concept for it was 'to explore the connection between birdsong and light, and why the light triggers the birds to sing.'[6] When it came time to develop the work into a theatrical presentation, she needed to flesh out the story, as she mused in the programme, '*Ninth Wave* was pretty easy to put together but *Sky of Honey*, like the feel of the piece, was the complete opposite . . . What was the action on stage to be? It needed a great deal of "stillness" in between flurries of movement that would gradually build up to all hell breaking loose.' And so *Aerial*'s hypnogogic, slightly stoned and surreal conceptual piece was tweaked for dramatic effect in *Before The Dawn*. The role of the Painter (who appears on two songs) became larger, a 'kind of "Pan" figure' who controls the weather and events on stage. It was conceived especially for Bertie. Also new, a wooden puppet in the shape of an artist's model that wanders around, interacting with various aspects of the set 'like a puppy . . . full of life and instinct'. Eventually, '[they'll be] the only one not caught up in the spell that is cast'.[7]

Act 3 begins with Bush at the piano seated among the band, surrounded by images of a silver-birch forest, calling to mind the dream sequence from the 'Suspended in Gaffa' music video (1982) and also the enchanted forest she sashayed through in 'The Sensual World' (1989). 'Prologue' moves as patiently as the slow-motion birds in flight that fill the entire rear wall of the stage, transitioning from hushed stillness to a euphoric crescendo that chimes in harmony with Rouen's ringing bells ('Ring it! Shake it down! Bring it on! Let it in!').

The songs transition from one to the next in gliding, graceful movements. A psychedelic, ever-shifting canvas appears, framing the sky for 'An Architect's Dream' and 'The Painter's Link'. The musicians stretch out on 'Sunset', which is something of a showcase for percussionist Cinélu, whose infectious rhythms drive the energy 'all the way up to the top of the night'. As the light turns to red and rust, magic is felt lurking in the liminal spaces 'Somewhere in Between'. As night falls, darker, more mysterious sonic colours come to play with new composition 'Tawny Moon'. A mystical ode to 'My love, my Luna, queen of bedlam', it's sung by the Painter (Bertie). The music consciously evokes some of the tell-tale aesthetics of *Hounds Of Love*-era Bush production: repeating, 'Page-R'-style Fairlight patterns; conspicuously synthetic, 'Cloudbusting'-style string samples; heavily gated electronic drums in the opening verse; the plucky, hard-panned 'Watching You Without Me'-style texture that cuts in during the bridge; the low-resolution sampled owl effects in the chorus. Could 'Tawny Moon' be a lost mid-1980s composition rescued from the vault? My research has been inconclusive, but Rosabel, I want to believe.

'Nocturn' brings the dramatic action back to the land of dreams. Diving 'deeper and deeper' into her imagined night swim, she encounters the helpless blackbird from 'Waking the Witch', while arcane rattles signal a shift to the muted riff from *The Ninth Wave*. The cross-pollination of the blackbird dream across acts deepens the possible readings – recurring images of fire, bells, blackbirds, magic and light, binding the tripartite experience into a cohesive whole. The troubling flashback resolves with the awed sight of the sunrise. *Before The Dawn* reaches an apex of power with its finale, 'Aerial', whipping up a sonic squall to rival the tempest of 'King of the Mountain'. With voltaic rhythms pulsating and ever-pushing, the whole venue feels the deeply primal, heart-thumping compulsion to join the birds in their dawn chorus. In the chaos, the puppet breaks free from its master, and silver-birch trees crash down from the sky, one of them skewering the grand piano, as feathers float down from the ceiling. A shamanic 'blackbird spirit' dances feverishly in shadows as Bush faces off against David Rhodes, who is wearing a frightening bird-skull mask. In the final moments, she laughs like a crow, rising many feet up into the air like The Morrígan, her beautiful black wings outstretched.

After a seemingly endless ovation, Bush returns to the stage alone to perform her first encore, a solo rendition of 'Among Angels' (*50 Words For Snow*, 2011). The grand piano she plays still has a great tree sticking through its middle. When she sings 'I can see angels around you' to the hushed room, it is as though she is addressing the very same entities summoned for protection, hers and ours, at the start. Finally, the entire Fellowship joins a rousing singalong to 'Cloudbusting' to bring the evening to a close. Shell-shocked and high on magic, my friend and I stagger towards Hammersmith tube station. I try to speak, but no sound comes out. I am dumbfounded. Melted to a puddle.

Reviews overwhelmingly gushed. 'Mesmeric' (*NME*). 'Spellbindingly beautiful' (*Daily Mail*). 'Mind-bending' (BBC). *Billboard* called it 'sublime', the slightly confused Richard Smirke adding, 'What does it all mean? Who knows, but it's certainly more entertaining than watching your standard veteran act going through the motions for a reunion tour paycheck.' Special praise was saved for *The Ninth Wave* in *The Guardian*. Alexis Petridis observed that the staging had an 'astonishing effect, bolstering rather than overwhelming the emotional impact of the songs'.

The experience had an emotional impact on the artist, too. In a message posted on her website a few weeks after the final show, she wrote, 'I just never imagined it would be possible to connect with an audience on such a powerful and intimate level; to feel such, well quite frankly, love.' Fellowship member Jo Servi reflected on this powerful sense of intimacy in a social media post, saying, 'the venue is so intimate that you really can see the expressions on people's faces. The joy, the elation, the thanks, people cry.'

Sound engineer Stephen W Tayler, fresh from working with Bush on *Director's Cut* and *50 Words For Snow*, was put in charge of her vocals and effects (credited in the programme as 'Kate Vocal Navigator'). He told me about the unique tension he and the crew felt delivering such a technically intricate presentation to a hungry, emotional crowd. 'Every night, when the show started, the audience exploded. I just remember everybody on the production was on edge the whole time. Nobody could relax until the encore arrived.' Tayler's job was to handle the vast array of special effects applied to Bush's live vocal ('I was her human effects pedal'), in addition to controlling the sound of her voice and what she could hear via in-ear monitors. The approach was more like how an engineer would track a vocal recording in a studio. For an artist who felt far more comfortable in the studio than on stage, Bush was thankful, acknowledging him in the programme ('[Tayler's work] has given me huge amounts of confidence'). They worked together again to mix the *Before The Dawn* live album, an arduous process that involved sifting through twenty-two individual performances of twenty-nine separate pieces. The three-CD package, dubbed 'The KT Fellowship Presents *Before The Dawn*', arrived in 2016, and to date remains the only full, official document of the show.

Blackbirds

Lon dubh, our friendly garden songsters, are easy enough to spot. They can often be seen hopping about on British lawns, searching for delicious earthworms. If you're very lucky, you might catch one sunbathing, dozing, wings outstretched. More often, you might hear them before you see them; their languid song can be heard on the air at dawn and dusk, especially on those long, warm summer evenings, when the blackbird is likely to grant an extended performance.

In ancient Celtic stories, birds with black feathers – blackbirds but also corvids like ravens, crows, choughs and jackdaws – are the symbolic keepers of transitional realms, the places between light and dark, sunset and the new dawn, death and rebirth. Myths of The Morrígan, Rhiannon and Derg Corra feature prominent roles for these onyx avians. Celtic legends say if you put a blackbird's feather under someone's pillow, they will reveal their innermost secrets. But you don't need to believe in myths or superstitions to appreciate the magic of the blackbird: listen at dusk for their song of summer, the song of colours. For those who enjoy blackbird-spotting, Kate Bush's body of work contains a few:

1980: in Nick Price's Bosch-like cover for *Never for Ever*, a blackbird can be seen flying out from under her skirt, with musical notes trailing in its wake.

1985: in 'Waking the Witch' from *The Ninth Wave*, the image of a blackbird is evoked as part of the ducking trial. As the woman lost at sea is accused of witchcraft, she cries, 'Help this blackbird!', imagery that's possibly drawn from *The Witch of Blackbird Pond*.

1989/2016: two striking portraits from *The Sensual World*'s photoshoot by Guido Harari were manipulated many years later to include iridescent black plumage decorating Bush's face and hair. Harari named these images 'Wings' and 'Birdfish', in 2016.

1993: an early demo of 'Why Should I Love You?', the penultimate track on *The Red Shoes*, was leaked online in 2007. It has a lyric about blackbirds that was replaced in the final version:

'If I could sing like a blackbird, just like my heart was
    filled with summer

Of all the people in the world why should I love you?'

1993: for a set of promotional photos for *The Red Shoes* taken by Anthony Crickmay, Bush wears a black and red gown, its bodice decorated with iridescent feathers. A blackbird is positioned on her head like a fascinator hat.

1993: in the music video for 'And So Is Love', also in *The Line, the Cross & the Curve*, Bush encounters a trapped blackbird in her darkened dance studio; she catches and releases it, but it hits a glass window and dies. She picks up its body and kisses it to sleep. When she enters the mirror world to break the curse of the red shoes, she is dressed in the feathered gown from the Crickmay shoot, the blackbird placed in her hair, its wings pointing up.

1996: lyricist Don Black tells the following anecdote about Bush on an edition of the BBC Radio 2 programme *They Write the Songs*:

> I met Kate just a few weeks ago . . . I asked [her] if she had a favourite singer and she said her favourite is the blackbird and her second favourite is the thrush – well, I told you she was different.[1]

2005: the cover of *Aerial* might appear at first glance to be a rocky island landscape reflecting upon an oceanic horizon, but in fact the image is a waveform representation of blackbird song. This sound is heard often on the second disc of *Aerial* and its suite of pieces, known as *A Sky of Honey*: 'Prelude', 'Sunset', 'Aerial Tal' (where Bush mimics the bird's song in the style of Indian tala music) and the title-track finale, where a blackbird is given an entire section of the song to sing solo, with Bush laughing along.

In her 2005 *Mojo* interview, Bush says of blackbirds: 'It's almost like they're vocalising light . . . And I love the idea that it's a language we don't understand. Obviously, a lot of it is like, "Fuck off! This is my spot." And obviously, "Cor, you're a bit of all right!" But there's more to it than that. It's incredibly complex.'[2]

2011: the fourth word for snow on the title track from *50 Words For Snow* is 'Blackbird Braille'.

2014: blackbirds feature repeatedly in *Before The Dawn*, with the blackbird from *The Ninth Wave* narratively linked to the one in *A Sky of Honey*. Bush is seen wearing black wings momentarily at the end of 'Waking the Witch' and again at the gig's conclusion, when in the final seconds of 'Aerial' she takes flight.

Wave after wave

Owen Myers: You're often cited as an influence by contemporary artists, from Björk to Solange, and hip-hop artists like Big Boi from Outkast. What do you hope that other artists are able to take away from your work?

Kate Bush: I'm just so delighted if they like my work. And the more diverse [they are], the more exciting it is for me.
– Interview with Kate Bush, *The Fader*, 2016[1]

As I write this, it has been more than thirty-eight years since the release of *Hounds Of Love*. It's a pop-historical monument; visionary, complex yet still accessible, a high watermark in Kate Bush's career, an ethereal masterpiece by all critical consensus. And yet this middle-aged record still vibrates with freshness in the continually evolving zeitgeist. Perhaps that feeling has been buoyed by the late success of 'Running Up That Hill' in 2022 and the subsequent discovery of Bush's music by younger generations. But it's also true that the reason *Hounds Of Love* remains so vital in the present is because artists from every successive musical generation since it came out have carried its influence and embedded its legacy into the cultural fabric.

Its impact on self-producing singer-songwriters, particularly non-male ones, has been seismic. The stunning triumph of *Hounds Of Love* cleared a path for future would-be innovators who now had less to fear from being labelled 'eccentric' or 'hysterical' by the misogynistic music press. Bush's stubbornness in advocating for herself, her vision and her preferred ways of working kicked the doors open for artists coming after her to exist and create on their own terms. Her imagistic songwriting and immersive productions stretched the boundaries of what pop music could be. Writer Dorian Lynskey put it this way: 'Some artists open the door to a new room in the house of music; Bush is one of a handful whose imagination revealed the existence of a whole new wing.'[2]

When Tori Amos released her debut solo album *Little Earthquakes* in 1992, critics were quick to point out the similarities in her sound to that of Bush. Some of the comparisons made were lazy, as if pointing out the fact that both artists were mezzo-soprano singer-songwriters who also played piano was proof of a theft. Tom Doyle asked Amos about these comparisons in a 1998 *Q* interview, saying, 'So you were never influenced by [Bush] directly?', to which she responded, 'Well . . . I must tell you that when I heard her, I was blown away by her. There's no question.'[3] Listening to *Little Earthquakes*, which Amos co-produced, there is an undeniable *Hounds Of Love* quality to the big, gated percussion on 'Precious Things' and 'Crucify', with the latter song's melismatic 'Cha-ee-a-ee-a-ee-a-ee-ains' recalling something of the 'Yeah-ee-yeah-ee-yeah-eeee, yooo' from 'Cloudbusting'. That song's baroque-synthetic string arrangement feels echoed on Amos's 'Girl', and there is a 'Hello Earth' feeling to the chilly vocal production and orchestral sweep of 'China'. In *Q*, Doyle pointed out that *Little Earthquakes* would, in turn, be hugely influential ('the kook rock torch passed from Bush to Amos') in inspiring Alanis Morissette's 1995 breakthrough *Jagged Little Pill*. In another 1998 interview, with German outlet *Musikexpress*, Amos explained how listening to *The Ninth Wave* had inspired her to be brave in her life, saying '[*The Ninth Wave*] turned me inside out. It changed my life . . . I left the man I was living with because of this record.'[4] In addition to regularly including Bush covers in her sets ('Running Up That Hill', 'And Dream of Sheep'), in 2014 Amos appeared alongside a cavalcade of celebrity talking heads (including Elton John, Dave Gilmour, Neil Gaiman, Nigel Kennedy, Stephen Fry, John Lydon, St. Vincent, Tricky, Big Boi and more) praising Bush's legacy in the BBC documentary *The Kate Bush Story: Running Up That Hill*.

But to trace the influential waves of *Hounds Of Love*, one must look beyond Amos and her fellow Bush-loving successors (Fiona Apple, Regina Spektor, Cat Power, Natasha Khan aka Bat for Lashes, Florence + The Machine, Annie Clark aka St. Vincent, Taylor Swift) to the ground broken by self-producing, tech-adopting artists such as Björk, Imogen Heap, Karin Dreijer (The Knife, Fever Ray) and Grimes. Heap cited Bush as being one of the reasons labels took her work seriously, saying, 'Kate produced some truly outstanding music in an era dominated by men and gave us gals a licence to not just be "a bird who could sing and write a bit", which was the attitude of most execs'.[5] For DIY artists wishing to control every aspect of their presentation, from studio construction to image curation, Bush was a vital role model. In a 2016 interview, Grimes named her two biggest musical inspirations as Trent Reznor and Bush, '[two] people who have done what I like to think I'm doing'. She described her creative approach as a 'one-man show . . . I oversee everything myself; I produce and engineer and write everything . . . I do all of the visual artwork.'[6] In 2019, Grimes campaigned for the recognition of 'ethereal' as an official genre on streaming platforms and radio playlists, saying, 'we argue that there is a long lineage of auteur artists, often producing their own music and/or directing their own music videos . . . often very ethereal, otherworldly, and futuristic in nature'.[7] In 2021, Spotify recognized the term as a genre and partnered with Grimes to create a seven-and-a-half-hour playlist 'dedicated to experimentalism with strong elements of pop and universal beauty'. 'Running Up That Hill' was featured there, alongside work from artists such as FKA twigs, Caroline Polachek, Sophie, James Blake and Imogen Heap. The long line of 'ethereal auteurs' that Grimes advocates for and identifies with can be traced back to the pioneering work on *Hounds Of Love*. Bush's appeal in this group is not only about creative autonomy but also emotionally articulate artistry. Norwegian singer-songwriter, producer and author Jenny Hval (who published her master's thesis on Bush in 2011) praised Bush's ability to bring 'emotional density' to her songwriting via 'her voice, production twists and magnificent melodic themes. It's as if she is a reporter, reporting from the war zone of human experience.'[8] Fellow 'ethereal auteur' Julia Holter appeared on the popular podcast *Classic Album*

Sundays alongside Outkast's Big Boi (a superfan who inducted Bush into the Rock & Roll Hall of Fame in 2023) to discuss her admiration for *Hounds Of Love*, saying '[Bush's] music holds the emotional complexity of life.'[9]

The album's influence extends to rock bands, too. Brian Molko (Placebo) said that the album 'blew [his] mind completely', adding:

> It was the first time I'd heard a record that had such sonic unity to it . . . Kate created her own emotional universe. I'm nostalgic for that period in music because I think we're given too much information today, so there's less capacity for us to create those personal universes through somebody else's work. Kate's music meant I could leave the drudgery of my everyday life.[10]

Brett Anderson (Suede) cited Bush (alongside Bowie) as a major influence, telling *The Guardian* in 2013 that *Hounds Of Love* was 'the album that made me want to make albums', adding '[Suede's second album, 1994's] *Dog Man Star* wouldn't have been the same album without *Hounds Of Love* – it was totally inspired by it.'[11] Singer-songwriter and composer Rufus Wainwright was transparent in a 2005 interview with *Mojo* about Bush's influence on his work, saying,

> There a real danger that you become clouded when you listen to her. So many people try to copy her – no names, except for me! I've copied her . . . And I intend to copy her more! . . . Her attitude towards love and society's treatment of love is very combative and most gay people can connect with that.[12]

For Anohni (Anohni and the Johnsons), Bush was her 'first singer' ('sensuous and very pagan'[13]), who inspired, alongside Alison Moyet and Nina Simone, the development of her unique vocal style. In a 2023 interview with Björk, the two artists discussed Bush's influence on their work, with Björk simply identifying Bush as 'mother'.[14]

Björk's creative autonomy as a self-producing artist of texturally rich, concept-driven avant-pop owes much to Bush's legacy. She has always been quick to speak about her love of Bush's music, and the influence it has had on her creativity throughout her career, and her evolving aesthetic, inspired equally by a deep love of technology and enchantment with the natural world. Bush's belated commercial success in 2022 in the wake of *Stranger Things* was cited by Björk during promotional interviews leading up to the release of her tenth studio album, *Fossora*. The singer said that the moment was a triumph for female self-producing artists and a vindication for years of Bush enduring the sexist labelling of being 'insane' and a 'crazy witch'[15]. She continued:

> I'm really blushing. Do you think something of it has to do with the world finally being ready for matriarch music? I was just so happy for Kate Bush to get that international hit, 'Running Up That Hill'. I'm not saying we're going to take over, but I feel like all the hidden matriarchs out there are just crying: *Finally, we don't have to hide . . .* [Bush] was the *only* thing. It was her who was doing that. Everything else was patriarchy. [She laughs] I'm sorry, I'm exaggerating – but she was the producer, she was making

the environment she was singing in. That, for me, is the most matriarch environment. And I feel like the world, and Gen Z-ers – they're ready for it.

- Björk, Pitchfork, September 2022[16]

Both Björk and Bush were included in Solange Knowles's redefinition of the term 'classic'. 'We get to define our own terms and for me it's just about authenticity', she said, adding, 'they're Björk, Kate Bush, Erykah Badu. You can look at images or hear any part of their work now from 20 years ago and it's classic because it's authentically who they are, what they were, and what they were embodying.'[17] Solange performed a cover of 'Cloudbusting' at a number of appearances in 2014.

Even though I am not a famous musician, the influence of *Hounds Of Love* has been profound in my creative life. The album gives you permission to work the way you know how – the way you know is best. To follow your muse uncompromisingly. To give creative labour only on your own terms. It is a reminder that having a safe space, and privacy, is crucial. It also reinforces the value of working slowly – that slow work can still engage with our intuitive senses. The length of time between *Hounds Of Love* and what came next only dilates – four years until *The Sensual World* (1989), another four to *The Red Shoes* (1993), a twelve-year gap to *Aerial* (2005), her late masterpiece, and another six years before *50 Words For Snow* (2011). The freedom to take one's time is a vital ingredient, and those gaps between records, not to mention the records themselves – all self-produced – would not have been possible without *Hounds*

Of Love. Nearly four decades on, it remains as sticky as ever in the culture, re-entering the public consciousness in consistent waves over generations: in 1992, Utah Saints sampled 'Cloudbusting' in their top five UK hit 'Something Good'; in 2003, Placebo covered 'Running Up That Hill', with their version synced in several TV shows; in 2005, indie band The Futureheads had a top 10 hit in the UK with their cover of 'Hounds of Love'; in 2012, a remix of 'Running Up That Hill', created specially for the London Olympics' closing ceremony, peaked at number six in the UK chart. In addition to the original song re-entering the charts in the wake of *Stranger Things* in 2022, it was also covered by German pop star Kim Petras, who is trans, and released to coincide with Pride Month celebrations. In a statement, Petras highlighted the song's LGBTQ+ credentials, saying, 'I have always been obsessed with "Running Up That Hill" . . . For me, it's about equality.'[18] All evidence suggests that *Hounds Of Love* will continue to remain relevant, resonant and alive. Its beauty and generosity are timeless. Its message of love's triumph over pain, isolation and darkness is something we need to hear, to *feel*, now more than ever.

Notes

Introduction

1 Walters, Barry. 2016. 'Hounds of Love'. Pitchfork, June.

2 Swales, Peter. 1985. 'Kate Bush'. *Musician*, Autumn.

3 Doyle, Tom. 2005. '"Weak? Frail? Mentally Unstable? Fuck Off!"' *Mojo*, December.

4 Skinner, Richard. 1992. *Classic Albums: Hounds Of Love*. BBC Radio 1, January.

5 Bush, Kate. 2022. 'Merry Christmas'. 20 December.

6 Bush, Kate. 2023. 'War Child – 1994'.

7 McIntyre, Hugh. 2022. '"Stranger Things" Music Supervisor Nora Felder Talks Helping Kate Bush Score an Unlikely Hit: Interview'. *Forbes*, 11 August.

8 Vermorel, Fred. 1983. *The Secret History of Kate Bush (and the Strange Art of Pop)*. London: Omnibus, p. 12.

9 MuchMusic. 1994. *Egos & Icons*. BCE Inc.

Still dreaming

1   Sinclair, David. 1994. 'Dear Diary: The Secret World of Kate Bush'. *Rolling Stone*, February.

2   Thomson, Graeme. (2010) 2015. *Under the Ivy: The Life and Music of Kate Bush*. London: Omnibus, p. 40.

3   *Lionheart* Promo Cassette, EMI Canada, 1978.

4   Diliberto, John. 1985. 'Britain's Renaissance Woman of Concept Rock'. *Keyboard*, July.

5   Bath, quoted in Thomson. *Under the Ivy*, p. 168.

6   Needs, Kris. 1980. 'Fire in the Bush'. *Zigzag*, August.

7   Boycott, Rosie. 1982. 'The Discreet Charm of Kate Bush'. *Company*, January.

8   Shearlaw, John. 1981. 'The Shock of the New'. *Record Mirror*, September.

9   Boycott. 'The Discreet Charm of Kate Bush'.

10 Hardiman, quoted in Thomson. *Under the Ivy*, p. 189.

11 Marvick, Andrew (ed.). 1984. *The Women of Rock*.

12 Blake, Mark. 2011. 'Cash for Questions: Peter Gabriel'. *Q*, December.

13 Sutherland, Steve. 1981. *Melody Maker*, July.

14 Starr, Red. 1981. *Smash Hits*, July.

15 Rouse, Rose. 1982. *Sounds*, September.

16 Tennant, Neil. 1982. *Smash Hits*, November.

17 White, Chris. 1983. *Music Week*, January.

18 Burton, Nick. 1983. *Record*, January.

19 Davis, Michael. 1983. *Creem*, March.

20 Skinner. *Classic Albums: Hounds Of Love*.

21 Bush, Kate. 2023. 'Hounds of Love'.

22 Doyle. "'Weak? Frail? Mentally Unstable? Fuck Off!'"

23 Solanas, Jane. 1985. 'Krufts Original!' *NME*, September.

24 Diliberto. 'Britain's Renaissance Woman of Concept Rock'.

25 Reynolds, Simon. 2014. 'Kate Bush, the Queen of Art-Pop who Defied her Critics'. *The Guardian*, August.

26 Myrdal, Jay. 2018. Quoted in 'The Story Behind the Iconic "Kite" Cover Artwork'. *Katebushnews.com*, February.

I put this moment . . . here

1 Hernandez, Karla, Smith, Dr Stacy L. and Piper, Dr Katherine. 2022. *Inclusion in the Recording Studio? Gender and Race/Ethnicity of Artists, Songwriters & Producers across 1,000 Popular Songs from 2012-2021*. USC Annenberg.

2 Diliberto. 'Britain's Renaissance Woman of Concept Rock'.

3 Horkins, Tony. 1985. 'What Katy Did'. *International Musician and Recording World*, October.

4 Nico, Ted. 1985. 'Fairy Tales & Nursery Rhymes'. *Melody Maker*, August.

5 MuchMusic. *Egos & Icons*.

6 Buskin, Richard. 1993. 'Del Palmer: The Red Shoes Sessions'. *Sound on Sound*, vol. nine, no. 2.

7 Horkins. 'What Katy Did'.

8 Glover, quoted in Thomson. *Under the Ivy*, p. 212.

9 Swales. 'Kate Bush'.

10 Marck, James. 1985. 'Kate Bush Breaks Out: Bush's Bridges'. *Toronto Weekly*, November.

11 Diliberto. 'Britain's Renaissance Woman of Concept Rock'.

12 Ibid.

13 Horkins. 'What Katy Did'.

14 Ibid.

15 Bell, Max. 1985. 'What Kate Bush Did Next'. *Sunday Express*, Autumn.

16 Bush, John Carder. 2015. *Kate: Inside the Rainbow*. Sphere.

17 Power, Ed. 2018. 'Kate Bush's Former Partner Fondly Recalls Visits to Ireland at Height of Fame'. *Irish Examiner*, October.

18 Skinner. *Classic Albums: Hounds Of Love*.

19 Swales. 'Kate Bush'.

20 Buskin. 'Del Palmer: The Red Shoes Sessions'.

21 Cooper, quoted in Thomson. *Under the Ivy*, p. 219.

22 Skinner. *Classic Albums: Hounds Of Love*.

Hounds Of Love

1 Myatt, Tony. 1985. Interview at the Kate Bush Convention, November.

2 Nicholls, Mike. 1985. 'The Girl Who Reached Wuthering Heights'. *The Times*, August.

3 MuchMusic. *Egos & Icons*.

4 Skinner. *Classic Albums: Hounds Of Love*.

5 Amplified. 2023. *The Hounds Run Up the Hill*. YouTube.

6   Doyle, Tom. 2022. *Running Up That Hill: 50 Visions of Kate Bush*. London: Nine Eight Books, p. 175.

7   Ibid., p. 174.

8   Myatt. Interview at the Kate Bush Convention.

9   Bush, Kate. 1985. Message to Kate Bush Club Newsletter, issue 18.

10 Unknown interviewer. 1985. 'What Kate Did Next'; quote reprinted in 'The Making of Kate Bush's Hounds of Love'. *Prog*, issue 44, 2014.

11 Sinclair, Paul. 2016. 'Guitarist David Rhodes on Performing with Kate Bush in Before The Dawn'. Super Deluxe Edition.

12 Skinner. *Classic Albums: Hounds Of Love*.

13 Bush. Message to Kate Bush Club Newsletter, issue 18.

14 Skinner. *Classic Albums: Hounds Of Love*.

15 Ibid.

The Ninth Wave

1   Bush, Kate. 1978. 'The Kick Inside'. De Efteling TV Special, TROS, the Netherlands.

2   Kruse, Holly. 1990. 'In Praise of Kate Bush'. In: *On Record: Pop, Rock and the Written Word*. Eds. Frith, Simon and Goodwin, Andrew. London: Routledge, pp. 450–65.

3   Fortune, Dion. (1934) 2000. *Glastonbury: Avalon of the Heart*. Newburyport, MA: Weiser Books, pp. 81–2.

4   Needs, Kris. 1985. 'Lassie'. *ZigZag*, November.

5   Jung, Carl. (1959) 2014. *The Archetypes and the Collective
    Unconscious*. In: *Collected Works*, vol. 9. New York: Routledge,
    p. 298.

6   Needs. 'Lassie'.

7   Skinner. *Classic Albums: Hounds Of Love*.

8   Bush, Kate. 1987. 'Cousin Kate: Interview with 'Zwort Finkle'.
    KBC, issue 21.

9   Skinner. *Classic Albums: Hounds Of Love*.

10 Buskin. 'Del Palmer: The Red Shoes Sessions'.

11 Kittredge, George Lyman. 1929. *Witchcraft in Old and New
    England*. Boston: Harvard University Press.

12 Bush, Kate. 2023. *How to Be Invisible*. London: Faber & Faber,
    pp. 164–5.

13 Skinner. *Classic Albums: Hounds Of Love*.

14 Doyle. *Running Up That Hill: 50 Visions of Kate Bush*,
    p.184.

15 Skinner. *Classic Albums: Hounds Of Love*.

16 Bush, Kate. 1985. 'Hounds of Love Songs'. *KBC*, issue 18.

17 Alan, Doug. 1985. 'Love-Hounds Interview.' November.

18 Ibid.

19 Skinner. *Classic Albums: Hounds Of Love*.

20 Wallechinsky, David and Wallace, Irving. 1975. *The People's
    Almanac*. Doubleday, p. 675.

    (Similar versions of this anecdote have been attributed to
    fellow Apollo astronauts Jim Lovell and Buzz Aldrin.)

21 Berkeley, Michael. 2005. 'Kate Bush Rules, OK?' *The
    Guardian*, October.

22 Jacobi, Jolande. 1959. *Complex/Archetype/Symbol in the Psychology of C.G. Jung.* Princeton: Princeton University Press, pp. 186–7.

23 Skinner. *Classic Albums: Hounds Of Love.*

24 Swales. 'Kate Bush'.

25 Doyle. *Running Up That Hill: 50 Visions of Kate Bush*, p. 175.

Before The Dawn

1 Marck, James. 1985. 'Kate Bush Breaks Out: Bush's Bridges'. *Toronto Weekly*, November.

2 Swales. 'Kate Bush'.

3 Bush, Kate. 2014. *Before The Dawn* programme. The KT Fellowship.

4 Swales. 'Kate Bush'.

5 Everitt, Matt and Savage, Mark. 2016. 'Kate Bush Recalls the "Terror" of Her 2014 Live Shows'. BBC, November.

6 Bush, Kate. 2016. *Before The Dawn*, CD liner notes. Fish People.

7 Bush. *Before The Dawn* programme.

Blackbirds

1 Black, Don. 1996. *They Write the Songs.* BBC Radio 2, July.

2 Doyle. '"Weak? Frail? Mentally Unstable? Fuck Off!"'.

Wave after wave

1   Myers. Owen. 2016. 'Kate Bush Speaks'. *The Fader*, November.

2   Lynskey, Dorian. 2022. 'Inside Kate Bush's Alternate Universe'. BBC, June.

3   Doyle, Tom. 1998. 'Ready Steady . . . Kook!' *Q*, May.

4   Amos, Tori. 1998. 'Mein Plattenschrank'. *Musikexpress/ Sounds*, April.

5   Smyth, David. 2014. 'Why We Love Kate Bush, by the Musicians She's Influenced'. *Evening Standard*, August.

6   Grimes. 2016. Interview with Grammy Pro at Lollapalooza festival. YouTube.

7   Grimes. 2019. Twitter/X.

8   Aroesti, Rachel. 2022. '"An Old Strain of English Magic Had Returned": Stars on Why They Fell in Love with Kate Bush'. *The Guardian*, July.

9   Murphy, Colleen. 2019. 'This Woman's Work: Hounds of Love by Kate Bush'. *Classic Album Sundays.*

10 Aroesti. '"An Old Strain of English Magic Had Returned": Stars on Why They Fell in Love with Kate Bush'.

11 Rogers, Jude. 2013. 'Brett Anderson: Soundtrack of my Life'. *The Guardian*, February.

12 Wainwright, quoted in Doyle. '"Weak? Frail? Mentally Unstable? Fuck Off!"'

13 Robinson, John. 2005. 'Music to His Ears'. *The Guardian*, November.

14 Björk. 2023. 'Anohni and Björk Talk Soul Music, Lou Reed, and Climate Collapse'. *Interview*, July.

15 Trendell, Andrew. 2022. 'Björk: "First You Create a Universe with Sound, Then You Move into it"'. *NME*, September.

16 Monroe, Jazz. 2022. 'Björk: Mother, Daughter, Force of Nature'. Pitchfork, September.

17 Ogunnaike, Nikki. 2017. 'Solange Wants to Redefine "Classic"'. *Elle*, April.

18 Petras, Kim. 2022. 'Running Up That Hill'. Press release.

Selected bibliography

Bush, John Carder. 2015. *Kate: Inside the Rainbow*. London: Sphere.

Bush, Kate. 2023. *How to Be Invisible*. London: Faber & Faber.

Doyle, Tom. 2022. *Running Up That Hill: 50 Visions of Kate Bush*. London: Nine Eight Books.

Fitzgerald-Morris, Krystyna, Fitzgerald-Morris, Peter and Cross, Dave (eds). 2014. *Homeground: The Kate Bush Magazine: Anthology One: 'Wuthering Heights' to 'The Sensual World'*. Maidstone, Kent: Crescent Moon Publishing.

Fortune, Dion (1930) 2011. *Psychic Self-Defense: The Classic Instruction Manual for Protecting Yourself Against Paranormal Attack*. Newburyport, MA: Weiser Books.

Jovanovic, Rob. 2005. *Kate Bush: The Biography*. London: Piatkus.

Kruse, Holly. 1990. 'In Praise of Kate Bush', in *On Record: Pop, Rock and the Written Word*. Eds. Frith, Simon and Goodwin, Andrew. London: Routledge.

Reich, Peter. (1972) 2019. *A Book of Dreams*. Reprint. London: John Blake.

Speare, Elizabeth George. 1958. *The Witch of Blackbird Pond*. New York: Clarion Books

Thomson, Graeme. (2010) 2015. *Under the Ivy: The Life and Music of Kate Bush*. London: Omnibus.

Webb, Mary. (1917) 1982. *Gone to Earth*. Leicester: Charnwood.

Young, Rob. 2010. *Electric Eden: Unearthing Britain's Visionary Music*. London: Faber.

Also Available in the Series

ALSO AVAILABLE IN THE SERIES

147. *Various Artists' I'm Your Fan: The Songs of Leonard Cohen* by Ray Padgett
148. *Janet Jackson's The Velvet Rope* by Ayanna Dozier
149. *Suicide's Suicide* by Andi Coulter
150. *Elvis Presley's From Elvis in Memphis* by Eric Wolfson
151. *Nick Cave and the Bad Seeds' Murder Ballads* by Santi Elijah Holley
152. *24 Carat Black's Ghetto: Misfortune's Wealth* by Zach Schonfeld
153. *Carole King's Tapestry* by Loren Glass
154. *Pearl Jam's Vs.* by Clint Brownlee
155. *Roxy Music's Avalon* by Simon Morrison
156. *Duran Duran's Rio* by Annie Zaleski
157. *Donna Summer's Once Upon a Time* by Alex Jeffery
158. *Sam Cooke's Live at the Harlem Square Club, 1963* by Colin Fleming
159. *Janelle Monáe's The ArchAndroid* by Alyssa Favreau
160. *John Prine's John Prine* by Erin Osmon
161. *Maria Callas's Lyric and Coloratura Arias* by Ginger Dellenbaugh

162. *The National's Boxer* by Ryan Pinkard
163. *Kraftwerk's Computer World* by Steve Tupai Francis
164. *Cat Power's Moon Pix* by Donna Kozloskie
165. *George Michael's Faith* by Matthew Horton
166. *Kendrick Lamar's To Pimp a Butterfly* by Sequoia Maner
167. *Britney Spears's Blackout* by Natasha Lasky
168. *Earth, Wind & Fire's That's the Way of the World* by Dwight E. Brooks
169. *Minnie Riperton's Come to My Garden* by Brittnay L. Proctor
170. *Babes in Toyland's Fontanelle* by Selena Chambers
171. *Madvillain's Madvillainy* by Will Hagle
172. *ESG's Come Away with ESG* by Cheri Percy
173. *BBC Radiophonic Workshop's BBC Radiophonic Workshop: A Retrospective* by William Weir
174. *Living Colour's Time's Up* by Kimberly Mack
175. *The Go-Go's Beauty and the Beat* by Lisa Whittington-Hill
176. *Madonna's Erotica* by Michael Dango
177. *Body Count's Body Count* by Ben Apatoff

143

178. *k.d. lang's Ingénue* by Joanna McNaney Stein

179. *Little Richard's Here's Little Richard* by Jordan Bassett

180. *Cardi B's Invasion of Privacy* by Ma'Chell Duma

181. *Pulp's This Is Hardcore* by Jane Savidge

182. *The Clash's Sandinista!* by Micajah Henley

183. *Depeche Mode's 101* by Mary Valle

184. *The Isley Brothers' 3+3* by Darrell M. McNeill

185. *Various Artists' Red Hot + Blue* by John S. Garrison

186. *Dolly Parton's White Limozeen* by Steacy Easton

187. *Garth Brooks' In the Life of Chris Gaines* by Stephen Deusner

188. *Kate Bush's Hounds of Love* by Leah Kardos